AN INTERACTIVE GUIDEBOOK FOR DESIGNING EDUCATION IN THE 21ST CENTURY

AN INTERACTIVE GUIDEBOOK FOR DESIGNING EDUCATION IN THE 21ST CENTURY

Or, John Dewey Never Said It Would Be Easy!

By
Jerrold E. Kemp, Ed.D.

TECHNOS Press of the Agency for Instructional Technology (AIT)
www.technos.net

In partnership with
Association for Educational Communications and Technology (AECT)
www.aect.org

Bloomington, Indiana

$22.95 U.S.
Published by TECHNOS Press of the Agency for Instructional Technology
in partnership with the Association for Educational Communications and Technology
Box A, Bloomington, IN 47402-0120
www.technos.net and *www.aect.org*

AIT Customer Service: 1-800-457-4509
www.ait.net

First Edition

ISBN 0-7842-0883-2

Library of Congress Catalog Card Number: 00-105902

AMY BOND, TECHNOS Press Coordinator, *Publication Coordinator*
PHILLIP HARRIS, Executive Director, Association for Educational Communications and
    Technology, *Developer*
LAURA LESLIE, Editor, AIT, *Assistant Editor*
CAROLE NOVAK, Manager of TECHNOS Press, *Editor*
DAVID STRANGE, Designer/Formatter, AIT, *Associate Editor and Compositor*
MICHAEL F. SULLIVAN, Executive Director, Agency for Instructional Technology, *Publisher*

Cover Illustration by SITUATIONAL MEDIA

Printed by Maple-Vail Book Manufacturing Group of The Maple Press Company, York,
Pennsylvania, USA

DEDICATION

When a person conceives an idea for a new venture, like writing a book, he or she sets goals and then structures the content. In this process, many of the beliefs and information presented would be based on the writer's experiences and aspirations. But behind the experiences and intentions are previous learning and knowledge, often obtained through contacts with former teachers, colleagues, and acquaintances. The convictions that have led to this book were acquired through the influence of and valuable past associations with:

- **Edgar Dale** of Ohio State University, who presented a "cone of experiences" in his textbook, *Audio-Visual Methods in Teaching* (1946), that organized learning into stages of doing, observing, and symbolizing

- **Charles F. Hoban** of Pennsylvania State University, who at a leadership conference stated the concept of applying systems thinking to instructional planning for education

- **James D. Finn** of the University of Southern California, who in numerous presentations and articles provided both theoretical and practical foundations for extending education beyond conventional Industrial Age principles and practices for our technological age

- **L. C. Larson** of Indiana University, who directed a very dynamic graduate program in instructional technology that provided students with a variety of meaningful experiences and associations with outstanding instructors

- **Harvey Frye** of Indiana University, a remarkable professor who not only provided students with a wealth of practical media production experiences but also successfully guided students toward expressing their creative talents

- **Richard B. Lewis** of San Jose State University, who directed the audiovisual service program for the university, was a competent mentor, and educational partner

- **Samuel N. Postlethwait** of Purdue University, who, as a botany professor, introduced teaching alternatives with an emphasis on student self-paced learning through an audio-tutorial method that provided a starting point for initiating various innovative instructional changes on all educational levels

My thanks to these gentlemen for their influences on my career and also for becoming colleagues.

—*Jerrold E. Kemp, Ed.D.*

ACKNOWLEDGMENTS

I recognize colleagues who have encouraged and assisted me with their reactions, advice, and suggestions concerning the content and its treatment in this book. Foremost have been Harold Hailer, who, in addition to teaching, served for many years as chair of the Department of Instructional Technology in the School of Education, San Jose State University; and Ron McBeath, Director of the Instructional Resources Center and the Faculty and Instructional Development Office at San Jose State, and professor in the Department of Instructional Technology. As you will see, Ron developed the Three-Stage Transformational Model of Change in Education, which serves as the perspective for the systematic instructional process presented in this book.

Among persons who reviewed early versions of this guidebook and offered thoughtful responses are Bob Hale, former media specialist, Connecticut State Department of Education; James Fryer, editor of the *California Curriculum News* (a publication of the California County Superintendents Educational Services Association); Al Mizell, Director of Technology, NOVA Southeastern University–FCAE; and Michael Molenda, professor of Instructional Systems Technology, Indiana University. Many other educators also received a trial version of the manuscript, providing evaluations and suggestions.

I also thank two long-time professional acquaintances for their assistance with the original content for the two appendices, "A School Changes" and "Students Make It Happen!": Maureen West, staff development coordinator for Math and Science, Santa Clara County Office of Education, San Jose; and Richard Ingalls, lead teacher/advisor for School Change, Bryson Avenue Schools, Los Angeles Unified School System, South Gate, California. Maureen and Rich very kindly devoted much time to reviewing the text, offering reactions and suggested improvements. These appendices are adapted from publications originally made for the Presidents' Library of the Association for Educational Communications and Technology (AECT).

The artwork in this book and the initial cover design were created by Ron Carraher, who, until recent retirement, was in the art department at the University of Washington. Ron started working with me in the early 1960s on my first publication, *Planning and Producing Audiovisual Materials.* Thanks, Ron, for the many creative pieces of clearly communicative art.

Although she is not active in my vocation, I owe a great deal to my wife Edith, who, with her own professional skills, served as a critic and helped to clarify some complex concepts with which I struggled.

And, finally, my appreciation to Joyce Sterling for her guidance and assistance in formatting the text and getting the book ready for publication.

—*Jerrold E. Kemp*
Mariposa, California
June 2000

TABLE OF CONTENTS

A model for educational change

A design plan
What makes a successful school?
A postscript

Analysis phase
Initiation phase
Development phase
Implementation phase
Final program evaluation phase

Colleagues as co-members of the planning team
Personal behaviors for planning
Ready to proceed?

School problems
Student learning needs and characteristics
Parent and community involvement with the school
Specifying needs

Continuing program expenses
Reactions to the program
Long-term benefits
Extension of the new program
Reporting results

Initiating the new program
Designing and implementing the program
Evaluating and managing the program
Transformation can work *if* . . .

Too few efforts to improve public education have provided positive results to cheer about. Principals and teachers, who are under constant pressure to attain successful student results on standardized tests and reduce problems in schools, need to give more systematic attention to comprehensive reforms of school programs.

We hear the term "educational accountability" being used more frequently. As Jean Allan, president of the Center for Educational Reform, stated, "Schools are still not accustomed to acting like businesses or needing to prove results" ("Baldridge Winners Named: No Awards in Health or Schools," *USA Today*, November 26, 1999, p. 3B).

Four factors are making accountability more important in public education:

- Rising educational requirements for good jobs while preparing a diverse and flexible workforce

- Limited degree of acceptable performance of graduates from many schools

- Need to control instructional costs while increasing learning effectiveness and efficiency

- Spread of school choice, which is giving a growing number of parents the option of selecting the best schools for their children to attend

To serve these accountability needs, a new design, leading to a restructuring or transformation of instruction, is necessary in keeping with social and economic needs of the 21st Century. This could build on much that good schools are now doing, but does require a fresh focus that starts with identified needs and seeks solutions in a comprehensive, orderly way. This procedure also recognizes organizational changes that become necessary within a school.

The goals for this interactive guidebook are:

- To provide an understanding that improving education by making systemic changes requires major shifts in our assumptions, beliefs, and actions.

- To encourage and guide administrators and teachers to apply a practical, cohesive plan, adaptable to their own situations, for transforming an instructional program to achieve successful results.

To accomplish these goals, the guidebook consists of two sections and two appendices:

- **Section One: Preparing Your Thoughts for Educational Transformation**—introduces a model for transformation that can guide the reader toward understanding the changes necessary in our thinking and our actions for the successful improvement of schools today.

- **Section Two: An Instructional Design Process and Procedures**—provides essential information for the development, support, implementation, evaluation, and extension of a systematically planned school restructuring program based on the model introduced in Section One.

- **Appendix A: A School Changes**—describes in a realistic situation how this school transformation process can be initiated and then implemented by a team of motivated teachers, with the coordination of the principal, the guidance of an instructional designer, and the involvement of parents and persons from the community.

- **Appendix B: Students Make It Happen!**—treats the same school situation introduced in

Appendix A from the students' positions by following two different students through the implementation of the new school program.

A key component of any change process is the people involved. Leadership, cooperation, and support are all necessary. This guidebook can be of value to anyone involved in or interested in school reform, whether for a project like integrating computers into a classroom, redesigning a single course, restructuring a whole department, or transforming a school's complete operation. These applications can be beneficial in a regular school, an alternative school, or a new charter school.

This book is directed to four major audiences:

- **teachers** who are interested in or actively involved in innovative school activities, with responsibilities for development, implementation, and evaluation of instructional programs

- educators who can serve as qualified **instructional designers** (possibly one of the above teachers) to guide the planning process to be described here

- **school principals, department heads, facilitators, and other administrators** who have leadership, organizational, managerial, and evaluative responsibilities for new or redesigned school development projects

- **professors of higher education courses** in school administration, teacher education, and instructional systems technology who wish to prepare education students for their new roles in 21st-Century schools

Second-level audiences for this book are persons who may have policy, leadership, support, or other interests in school transformation. They include:

- parents

- district and county superintendents and staff

- school board members

- state education department staff

- state and national legislators

- representatives of community organizations and businesses

Do you find yourself listed above? If not, please add yourself. You are welcome!

If you are a member of this second audience category, you may not be as interested in all the details of the comprehensive planning process presented here. For this reason, Chapter 4 provides a brief overview of the elements that are treated in detail in the chapters that follow. The appendices furnish an understanding of potential results for the systematic design process described. By reading the appendices *first*, you can see where we are going in a practical, school-transformational situation even before we start the journey!

The awareness and understanding you acquire can help with policy and operational decisions you may make, and will hopefully motivate you to become an active participant in a transformational school project.

Please note: The contents of this guidebook are presented in a useful, succinct manner. Rather than treating information in a lengthy paragraph format, I often use brief explanations and accompanying lists of helpful points or suggestions, each of which is numbered or starts with a bullet or other symbol. Some of these lists are necessarily lengthy. I hope you find this method to be a helpful way of briefly communicating useful information.

Also, as you progress through chapters, you will find *italicized* questions that relate to the content and that can encourage thoughtful actions or reactions by the reader. As appropriate, especially if you are a member of the main audience, try to respond. These interactions can guide you to beneficial decisions, actions, and efforts in your own situation. ◆

A VISION

Here is a school that reformed itself from the inside out by starting small and expanding the restructuring incrementally. Its philosophy is centered on teaching the whole child through learning-centered instruction, an integrated curriculum, and student mastery of basic skills. Parents, students, and teachers have developed a shared vision together. After careful consideration and detailed planning, new ideas are implemented gradually, including a variety of strategies that recognize individual style differences. With the principal, each teacher is considered a co-director of the school, having collaborative decision-making responsibilities. Students have a great say in their school. They are motivated, well behaved, and responsive, while learning the values of independent thinking. Any problem with a troublesome student is quickly faced and reasonably resolved. There is a strong volunteer presence in the school—staff, aides, library and learning lab assistants, and chaperones who help with field trips. Most parents participate in scheduled conferences with teachers.

The teachers' job has shifted from being dispensers of information to producers of environments that guide students to learn as much as possible by finding and managing the information they need or want. Most students come early to class (or even to school), stay after regular instruction ends, often work through lunch, and continue at home voluntarily. When active in a project, they have no motivational or disciplinary problems. Assistance comes through cooperation from other students almost as often as from the teacher or an aide.

Not only is more material covered than just the required curriculum, but it is treated in a shorter time than usual, and the students are learning more useful knowledge than ever before. Learning by students is based on measurements of individual progress according to agreed objective requirements. An atmosphere of energy, intensity, and pleasure, along with a sense of discovery and accomplishment are felt throughout the school.

Adapted in part from P. M. Senge, *The Fifth Discipline Fieldbook: Strategies and Tools for Building a Learning Organization,* New York: Doubleday (1990), pp. 489–490.

SECTION ONE

Preparing Your Thoughts for Educational Transformation

Chapter 1: Where Are We? . . . Where Should We Be Going?

Chapter 2: A Perspective for Educational Transformation

As indicated in the preface, in many chapters you will find questions in *italics* that encourage you to react to specific points of content. If you find the subject of this guidebook to be important and the information presented to be potentially useful in your professional work, it may be advantageous to have a separate notebook for answering the questions raised and entering reactions or other comments that are triggered by what you read. The entries can help in your own planning and development work. It can also be beneficial to share notes and remarks with colleagues.

CHAPTER 1

Where Are We? . . .
Where Should We Be Going?

Remember the slogan that was on a large poster in Democratic National Committee headquarters during the 1992 presidential campaign?—*It's the economy, stupid!* There should be a comparable slogan for public education today: *It's a new plan for instruction we need, my friends!*

This assertion can start to provide an answer to the question, "With all the attention being given to education, why has there not been more progress toward the necessary accomplishments that are wanted?" Various authorities challenge widely held assumptions about education and recognize the need for a fresh approach, based on more careful efforts, that can lead toward successful learning. Here are some of their views.

> If only one high school sophomore in ten passes the new standardized math test, as was the case in Arizona, the answer is not to make the test easier, as some parents, teachers, and administrators have asked the state's Board of Education to do. The answer is to do what's necessary to get our kids to the higher standards: **changes in teacher training, more rigorous curricula and instruction, better assessment that drives quality instruction and accountability.** [Emphasis added.]
>
> —Louis V. Gerstner, CEO of IBM, *USA Today*, January 3, 2000, p. 19A

Numerical goals, like those specified in *America 2000: An Educational Study*, published by the Secretary of Education (1991) and advocated by President George Bush, accomplish little. Ranking individual students, schools, and districts does not improve education. The question to answer is: **By what methods can education be transformed to improve learning?** [Emphasis added.]

> —W. E. Deming, *The New Economics*, Cambridge, MA: Massachusetts Institute of Technology, Center for Advanced Engineering Study (1993), p. 47

Sandra Cooney, director of the Middle Schools Education Initiatives at the Southern Regional Board, cautions middle schools against doing "the right things for the wrong reasons. They now have team teaching, block scheduling, advisory home rooms, and other typical middle school strategies. **But they haven't taken the next step and figured out how to use these components in ways that raise the achievement of all students.**" [Emphasis added.]

> —*USA Today*, October 6, 1998, pp. 1–2D

What is new in our time is an emerging knowledge based on the change process in schools and a growing understanding that **restructuring schools will require a comprehensive, integrated change of both the structure of the workplace of teaching and practices between teacher and student.** [Emphasis added.]

—A. Lieberman, ed.,
Building a Professional Culture in Schools, New York:
Teachers College Press, Columbia University (1988)

Simply making small changes for change's sake will not be enough. Already some schools and districts are in dangerous straits for having restructured, reorganized, and blindly installed site-based management programs, computer labs, or a thematic curriculum in the belief that these were some sort of "magic bullets" for improving results. These small reforms are akin to oiling the parts of a worn-out piece of machinery. **What is needed instead is to transform our current educational system into a totally different kind of enterprise. Such a transformation will require creative and productive thinking, planning, and work.** [Emphasis added.]

—D. F. Salisbury, *Five Technologies for Educational Change,* Englewood Cliffs, NJ:
Educational Technology Publications (1996), p. 4

From the above analyses, it can be seen that one key cause of the lack of student achievement is educators' inability to approach educational change in a fresh, all-inclusive way. Most often we base our decisions and actions on past experiences, with the expectation that something new should fit within established and accepted patterns. Is it not true that most people still think of education as conducted by a teacher standing at the front of a classroom, frequently talking and using a blackboard? They see students seated in rows, listening, and when directed, answering questions or reading from a textbook and completing workbook assignments. The usual goal has been to memorize information for tests, with resulting grades of A, B, C, D, or F.

Furthermore, because everyone has experienced the educational process, particularly in their youth, most laymen as well as educators believe they are knowledgeable about education and are qualified to recommend changes. But the world we live in today is appreciably different from that in which most of us experienced our education. No longer can education be considered in terms of former beliefs, assumptions, and needs. Therefore, we must give serious consideration to transforming the entire system of education.

Another important statement, this time from the workplace position, further substantiates the foregoing:

> When I started working 20 years ago, to build a product there was a single operation for each worker. You only had to memorize the task and do it repeatedly. But today I do many operations at one time. For one thing, you have to think before randomly pushing buttons and pulling switches. My job has broadened to include not only routine maintenance and service, but also equipment troubleshooting and debugging, even simple computer programming, with responsibilities for quality that require frequent decision making, and teamwork with other workers. We find our technology now changing so fast that continued training is necessary to cope with new tasks as they arise.
>
> Young people entering this world of work will be required not only to have computer skills, but also to think for themselves and take the initiative as needs arise. I know that behind these abilities are necessary competencies in basic math, reading, writing, and communicating clearly with other employees.
>
> Today high-wage manufacturing and comparable jobs in other areas can be very demanding and stimulating. **I hope the schools will prepare their students for this new world better than I was prepared for it.** [Emphasis added.]

—Adapted from P. S. Adler, *Technology and the Future of Work,* New York: Oxford University Press (1992)

The following observation summarizes the present situation, and indicates where we must go.

As we look back over the twentieth century, we see almost endless examples of educational experimentation and reform. Many have been cyclical, leaving little definitive evidence to either support their adoption or to encourage their abandonment. They generate only enough lasting interest to encourage new generations to try again. We have only tinkered with our system of education to bring about change.

But as the society has changed and knowledge continues to multiply, the urgency of educational reform becomes more pressing, and the negative consequences of retaining the status quo have long since passed any reasonable level of tolerance.

It is not new reforms that are needed, but an entirely new design and framework for educational transformation. Many of its supporting elements are already known but will remain insignificant until a new framework is put into place. [Emphasis added.]

—Adapted from D. W. Allen, *Schools for a New Century*, New York: Praeger (1992), p. 41

Finally, we so often hear and see proud declarations or pleas for excellence in education. During the 2000 political election season, politicians, in many speeches, expressed the need for revolutionary change in education. Most people have a fair idea about the goals and accomplishments desired for educating our youth, but if questioned about how to reach these desired levels, usually propose only limited, piecemeal solutions. Too often, simplistic solutions are recommended for complex problems, and it must be recognized that it takes more than money to improve education in our world today. Let me offer a more meaningful way to proceed. ◆

NOTES

CHAPTER 2

A Perspective for Educational Transformation

▶ *What are the beliefs and personal perspective that influence your understanding of the educational process today?*

The above question can help you to identify where you now fit philosophically within the educational process. Identify your own beliefs by answering each of the 12 questions below. Mark the answer that best represents your personal perspective.

1. How do you essentially view the educational process?
   a. as *autocratic*, controlled from the top down
   b. as *laissez-faire*, allowing educators to act without interference or direction
   c. as *democratic*, requiring equality and opportunity for both educators and students

2. How do you see the teacher's role in education?
   a. as *encouraging* student inquiry and problem solving
   b. as being *in charge*, dominating the classroom
   c. as being *permissive*, allowing students much freedom to select activities and set their own schedules

3. Which statement do you most readily accept?
   a. A teacher should do things *for* students.
   b. A teacher should do things *with* students.
   c. A teacher should do things *to* students.

4. A school curriculum should be structured with an emphasis on
   a. many *separate subjects*
   b. *methods* for all subject areas
   c. an *interdisciplinary* treatment of subjects

5. Teaching practices should be oriented toward
   a. the *presentation of subject matter*
   b. the *process of learning*
   c. the *performance of students*

6. Which method of student grouping do you prefer?
   a. by level of readiness for studying a topic or subject
   b. by *age*
   c. according to *preset standards*

7. How would you classify media resources available for teaching today?
   a. as *instructional technologies* integrated within teaching and learning methods
   b. as *teaching aids* to use, as time permits, in making presentations
   c. as *audiovisual techniques* for use to supplement verbal learning

8. What category of learning results is most important?
   a. *response mastery* for competency in using knowledge acquired
   b. *fixed responses* as required on objective-type tests
   c. *varied responses* depending on student's interests and accomplishments

9. Which category of thought process for student learning do you prefer?
   a. *logical and creative* thinking
   b. *logical* thinking and *free expression*
   c. *logical* thinking and *rote learning*

10. Which expression best represents the result of learning?
    a. students being *competitive* with each other
    b. students being *cooperative* with each other
    c. students recognizing learning as a challenging *adventure*

11. As an outcome of learning, students should be
    a. *self-actualizing*
    b. *inner-directed through traditional practices*
    c. *other-directed*

12. Another outcome of learning is to prepare students to be
    a. *independent*
    b. *interdependent*
    c. *dependent*

Although you may not be completely familiar with expressions used in some answers to these questions, you should recognize that, taken together, your answers fall within an educational pattern that reflects your beliefs about principles, practices, and outcomes of the educational process. Three patterns of educational change and transformation are identified as stages of transformation in Figure 1.

Using the notations beside the entries in Figure 1, find each answer you selected for questions 1–12. Then, beside each question, indicate the stage number (1, 2, or 3) under which your answer is found.

Do most, if not all, of your answers fit consistently within a single stage? It certainly is possible to select factors in more than one stage. But generally, in keeping with the pattern of your beliefs, you will probably have chosen a predominance of items grouped under one of the three stages. These stages represent three major patterns of educational philosophy comprising educational theory, principles, practices, and outcomes. By comparing the entries across each line, you can recognize the differences in beliefs and treatment of the concepts within each stage.

A MODEL FOR EDUCATIONAL CHANGE

Let us examine the three stages of educational change presented in Figure 1.

- **Stage 1** serves the needs of dependent, linear-thinking students. The acquisition and memorization of facts is a main task for these students. The student's mind is seen as a fishnet that will catch whatever is poured into it. It is assumed that the bigger nets (i.e., better minds) will catch more knowledge.

  The teacher, who holds a center position in the educational process, primarily directs students' learning through the textbook-and-lecture mode. Questions are asked to check that students are memorizing the correct information. Tests are mainly used to measure the recall of information provided. Scoring is objective, assessed according to a preset standard with grades assigned on the normal curve.

- **Stage 2** provides opportunities to improve learning conditions by making available alternative methods and materials for students who have various levels of experience and different learning styles. There may be some full-class teaching, but more time is spent in cooperative learning on small-group work and individual studies.

  The teacher provides different points of view and helps students to see the applications of the various positions. Tests are expanded from recall to application questions for the ideas studied. Discussions involving student experiences and individual opinions become important parts of the instructional program. Grading is a more subjective judgment by the teacher than in Stage 1.

- **Stage 3** provides learning experiences to encourage students, who now are at the center of the educational process, to explore, think creatively, and take risks in their educational activities. Students are helped to identify problems, gain understanding through their own efforts, and search for new ways of initiating inquiries. Not only does testing include recall, applications, implications, and creative explorations, it also is used diagnostically to help open further avenues for learning.

Rather than requiring competition among students, as in Stage 1, or allowing an open, laissez-faire approach, as in Stage 2, the educational change process in Stage 3 enables each student (or each group of students), with teacher guidance, to accept or set several of his or her own objectives. Most students can judge their own progress. A variety of evaluation methods determines individual accomplishments and performance competency.

As you consider these three stages, recognize that the beliefs and practices of teachers, administrators, parents, legislators, and others will place them in

FIGURE 1
A Model Depicting Educational Change as Sequential, Emergent, and Transformed

Stage 1	Stage 2	Stage 3
Principles		
Question		
1. **a.** autocratic passive mind linear thinking	**b.** laissez-faire independent mind open-ended attitude	**c.** democratic interactive mind pluralistic approach
Practices		
2. **b.** teacher-dominated	**c.** permissive	**a.** inquiry-centered
3. **c.** do things to	**a.** do things for	**b.** do things with
4. **a.** subject emphasis	**b.** method emphasis	**c.** interdisciplinary
5. **a.** product-oriented extrinsic manipulation	**b.** process-oriented random reinforcement	**c.** performance-oriented meaningful involvement
6. **c.** standards grouping class teaching fixed stimulus limited access limited resources	**b.** age grouping group teaching multiple stimuli random access multiple resources	**a.** readiness grouping independent study organized stimuli systematic access instructional systems
7. **a.** teaching aids	**b.** audiovisual techniques	**c.** instructional technologies
Outcomes		
8. **b.** fixed response	**c.** varied response	**a.** response mastery
9. **c.** convergent thinking and rote memory	**b.** convergent thinking and free expression	**a.** convergent thinking and divergent thinking
10. **a.** competitive	**b.** cooperative	**c.** adventure
11. **b.** inner-directed	**c.** other-directed	**a.** self-actualizing
12. **c.** dependent	**a.** independent	**b.** interdependent

Adapted from McBeath, "Is Education Becoming?" AudioVisual Communications Review *(Spring 1969), pp. 36–40).*

different stages according to the types of outcomes each individual feels should be achieved in an educational program. Unfortunately, the urgent need to prepare students to successfully achieve required learning standards often leads to Stage 1 teaching practices, and may dampen efforts to restructure educational programs. (See page 45 for consideration of the standards matter.) Also realize that the components listed under Stage 3 of the McBeath model do fit most educational needs of our students today who will live, work, and raise families in this emerging Information Age.

Since developing this model, Ron McBeath has presented it both nationally and internationally to numerous educational and lay groups. After explaining the details, he frequently asks this question: "Consider educators (administrators and teachers) with whom you work or whom you know. What percentage of them reveal beliefs or exhibit actual practices in each of the three stages?" Typically, results are close to:

Stage 1:   75%

Stage 2:   20%

Stage 3:   5%

These percentages clearly indicate a major problem faced by educators. The beliefs and practices of the great majority of educators remain in the past— the tradition of the teacher-centered, autocratic classroom. Extend this concept to parents, students, school boards, and legislators, who have important influences on and roles in education today. They no doubt also have Stage 1 ideas about how education should be conducted. (Recall the common picture of classroom instruction as described on page 8.) How many businesses can successfully function today with an Agricultural- or Industrial-Age perspective? It is essential that businesses and industries operate within Information-Age principles and practices for successful outcomes. (See publications by Boulding, Deming, Drucker, Naisbitt and Aburdene, Senge, and Toffler in "References and Sources," Section A, on page 165.)

The model that comprises Figure 1 was proposed by McBeath in 1969 (yes, that 31-year-old date is not a typo!):

The move in education today is away from autocratic and laissez-faire toward democratic control; doing things **to** and **for**, to doing things **with** students. Through this shift in control, responsible freedom for students is more attainable. It is significant that this move toward practices of readiness, involvement, and inquiry is most likely to produce outcomes such as response mastery, adventure, and self-actualization. These are all important for educating students in today's rapidly changing society.

The model shows that there should be growth toward a **systematic design of instruction** and [that it] is not just a matter of changing one or a number of discrete and isolated factors that affect the instructional and learning processes.

By thus relating many interdependent variables, the model highlights the way in which educational principles, practices, and outcomes are related to and determined by the emerging stages of change in our technological society.

—Adapted from "Is Education Becoming?" *Audio-Visual Communications Review* (Spring 1969), pp. 36–40

Do you recognize the practicality of the three-stage model in Figure 1 and agree with the rationale expressed by McBeath? Identify further where you place yourself, and recognize why there is so much dissonance and mismatch between the efforts of educators to restructure a program and the methods that should be used today that can lead to necessary outcomes.

The important questions for you now are:

- *Where do you want to be?*

- *What outcomes do you seek?*

- *What principles are needed to guide your practices?*

- *What skills and assistance do you need to implement the types of practices needed to achieve the desired outcomes?*

Answers to these questions require an orderly process that offers a practical way to decide on and accomplish the goals for any school or instructional program. The plans and procedures presented in this guidebook are focused on helping you to develop programs that will guide students toward Stage 3 outcomes. Hopefully, you are prepared for, or at least at this time receptive to, this approach, and are willing to explore the necessary paradigm shift.

Here is a final reference that summarizes the present situation in education and sets a direction for positive transformation:

> Our decade-long effort to reform U.S. education has failed. It has failed because it has not let go of an educational vision that is neither workable nor appropriate to today's needs. Until traditional assumptions about the nature and meaning of education are upset (and a new paradigm replaces outworn ones), good ideas will languish regardless of their appropriateness. Reform that seeks to correct symptoms without first addressing causes are doomed. Just as no amount of bailing could have kept the *Titanic* afloat, no amount of improved content can save our crumbling educational structure. To effect fundamental meaningful reforms, **all** educators must first be able to admit and agree that our traditional guiding vision of education is no longer relevant in a postindustrial, knowledge-based society. This admission and agreement are inevitable but, because of the discomfits of change, remain far from universal. Second, educators must accept, then build on the model that the needs of a new society demand. **Finally, when our schools do acknowledge education's new paradigm, they will need an ordered process of change that will enable them to exchange the patterns rooted in an antiquated structure of ideas for those needed to enact a new vision.** [Emphasis added]

—K. G. Wilson and B. Daviss, *Redesigning Education*, New York: Henry Holt (1994), p. 20 ◆

SECTION TWO

An Instructional Design Process and Procedures

As educators read the above chapter titles, they may feel confident that they are knowledgeable about many of these topics, often having studied them during teacher education and then applying them in teaching. Also, administrators and teachers who are involved with innovative school activities may believe they already use the components of systematic planning presented here. These opinions may be true. If so, for them the information here can be a reinforcement, review, and extension of what they now do. But experience has shown that in many situations, these beliefs are rarely substantiated. Few of these components of systematic planning receive the detailed attention and careful application that are necessary in comprehensive educational transformation situations.

Finally, I reemphasize two items mentioned in the preface. First, Chapter 4 contains a brief overview of the components of systematic planning that are introduced in Chapter 3 and are treated in detail in the chapters that follow. This overview provides concise explanations that can give you a useful perspective on the whole process. Second, the interactive features included in these chapters may encourage you to respond to the questions raised and activities suggested. They can help you better understand the content and relate it directly to your own situation.

Because there are close relations among components of the planning process to be described, you will find cross-references in one chapter to pages in another one. It can be useful to turn to the noted page for further information on the topic. Also, "References and Sources," listed at the end of the book, are frequently cited for your information if you would like more in-depth treatment of some subjects.

There are a number of other textbooks and references that treat instructional design concepts (see "References and Sources"), often with an emphasis on carefully explained theoretical and higher-order academic content, and containing applications that are mainly useful for improving training programs in business and industry. Hopefully, you will find the presentation here to be more in keeping with the practical knowledge needed on the school level.

CHAPTER 3

Setting the Stage for Successful Educational Transformation

▶ *Where should we start?*

▶ *What planning elements can provide specific, purposeful direction leading to successful student learning?*

We know that a school is a complex agency, influenced and directly affected by many factors, including social forces, state and federal statutes, politics, the local economy, and group or individual agendas, desires, and pressures. The process of education requires many interrelated elements that should all receive detailed attention. Neglecting or improperly treating any of them can lead to an unsatisfactory result.

Continuing with the last citation ending Chapter 2, a path to consider is indicated:

Luckily, industrial society has already perfected a process of continuous, guided innovation. Though children are not products, schools are not factories, and educators are not assembly-line workers, human energies can be organized to produce the consistent improvement and excellence that have been achieved in agriculture and in industry. When our schools embrace the vision and adopt similar strategies of change that other enterprises have pioneered, we will have taken the first step not only toward improving our schools but toward addressing the social dilemma that effective education alone can correct.

—K. G. Wilson and B. Daviss, *Redesigning Education,* New York: Henry Holt (1994), p. 20

Many non-education projects apply a **systems approach** to problem solving. Essentially, this is based on the **scientific method,** whereby a problem is recognized, a hypothesis is formed or a tentative solution is chosen, experiments are conducted, and data are gathered that lead to a conclusion about the accuracy of the hypothesis. This approach is conducted in an orderly, controlled manner that takes into consideration all necessary factors that can contribute to positive results. If successful, the results provide new knowledge, or are used to produce or improve the products of technology. If not fruitful, revisions or new plans are tried until success is realized. Thus, by adapting the scientific method, we have an *objective, systematic way of approaching educational problems.*

For training and education, this procedure becomes a comprehensive process for designing instruction. The term **instructional design** is commonly used when all components of systematic planning are treated in a coordinated manner. A qualified person who directs or coordinates this method of planning is called an **instructional designer** (see page 68).

For an education program, as for other applications, a system should be understood as a network of interdependent components that function together to accomplish a specific goal. (Note the term **instructional systems** under "Stage 3 Practices" in Figure 1 on page 9.) As stated in the introduction to Section Two, many educators believe they already develop and manage their instructional programs in this way. But upon carefully examining their plans and observing instructional procedures, we find "it ain't necessarily so." How decisions are made, objectives set, instructional and learning sequences created, resources selected, support provided, and learning evaluations performed: All are essential elements, and even if each one receives consideration, most are usually not treated in sufficient, integrated detail.

But there certainly are some teachers who do apply the slogan that opened Chapter 1—*It's a new plan for instruction we need, my friends.* They have designed successful, innovative programs that implement a procedure that to some degree is similar to what is proposed here. They are to be complimented and encouraged to continue and extend their efforts. (They probably are Stage 3 thinkers and implementers!) For example, the Nevada State Department of Education prepared *A Guide for Nevada Schools Planning: A Schoolwide Program* (1997). Although in a different format, this plan, along with details and participation activities, includes most of the analyzing, designing, and measuring components to be presented here. The Nevada approach certainly recognizes the need for a systematic method of change, shows that "it can be done." See "References and Sources," Section B, on pages 165–166 for other information and positions on the change process.

We now are prepared to ask this question:

▶ *How can we formulate an all-inclusive strategy for designing an educational program that potentially leads to improved quality of instruction, comprehensive high levels of ongoing student learning, and program success?*

A DESIGN PLAN

The answer to the above question requires a number of further operational questions within five major phases of a systematic and comprehensive plan. Each question is necessary, whether a single course is to be restructured, a cooperative project involves a team of teachers, or an entire school program is to be transformed.

Analysis phase

1. What are present **school problems** and **student learning needs** that provide the bases for reform and transformational change?

Initiation phase

2. How can a **vision statement** and **mission goals** be developed for the program?

3. What **priorities** and **constraints** for the program need recognition as the planning starts?

Developmental phase

4. What **curricula topics, basic skills, interdisciplinary themes,** and **other educational experiences** should comprise the instructional program?

5. What **subject content** supports each topic and theme?

6. In terms of subject content, what **learning objectives** should students attain for each topic or theme?

7. As determined by **pretesting,** what is the level of each student's preparation for studying a topic?

8. What **instructional methods** and **learning activities** can be used to accomplish the objectives?

9. What **instructional resources** are most suitable for carrying out instructional and learning activities?

10. What **logistical support** is required to initiate and maintain the instruction and learning?

11. How can **attainment of learning objectives** by students be determined?

Implementation phase

12. Do the results of a **program tryout** indicate need for any changes or improvements in order to meet expectations?

13. What other matters may need consideration when **implementing** and **managing** the new program?

Program evaluation and revision phase

14. After initial use, does the **program meet an acceptable level of learning competency** and other positive behaviors for subsequent use by other groups of students? If not, what revisions should be made?

15. Does the program operate in a **cost-effective** and **efficient** manner?

16. With success, can the program **be extended** within or even beyond the school?

This may appear to be a formidable list, but for an endeavor requiring major restructuring, careful attention should be given to all necessary components for a successful instructional program. And some items require consideration of a number of sub-elements. For instance, #10, logistical support, includes budget, facilities, materials, equipment, personnel responsibilities and training, and other essential services.

Figure 2 on the next page suggests an order for treating the elements represented by the 16 questions above. Note that there are no arrows directing the lines that lead from one box to another. Although a flow sequence is illustrated, feel free to treat the components in a flexible manner. Based on needs or the planning team's own preferences, a project can start at different places in the process, follow a preferred logical order, and even move back and forth. All elements are interrelated, so what you do in one component may cause changes in other ones already

developed. Because so many details require attention, the procedure by which you handle the treatment of these components can affect the ease and successful development of a school-improvement project. Refer to "The Mechanics of Planning" (pages 72–73) for guidance as you start this creative thought process.

While questions 1–12 guide a planning team in new program design, questions 13–16 are important to anyone having management or facilitation responsibilities for a major transformational program. Chapters 5 through 14 will show you how to develop successful answers to all these questions.

Keep in mind that choices to be made during the planning of these design components will be influenced by the following factors:

1. The information, skills, and attitudes needed for societal living and employment in the 21st Century.

2. Expanded knowledge about how learning can occur for a wide range of individual students.

3. A variety of instructional methods to provide for student learning.

4. An increasing array of technical resources that allow learning to be managed more efficiently and with more effective results.

5. The need to assess learning in multiple ways while both students and educators become accountable for the results.

WHAT MAKES A SUCCESSFUL SCHOOL?

In this book we examine a series of constructs that together can provide a satisfactory answer to this important question. As a starting point, let us recognize broad elements of a framework that is essential for successful instructional transformation in a school.

- An orientation toward the needs of the Information Age.

- An active, involved community, consisting of participating parents, teachers, students, and others.

(Continued on page 19)

FIGURE 2
Elements of Systematic Planning for Instruction

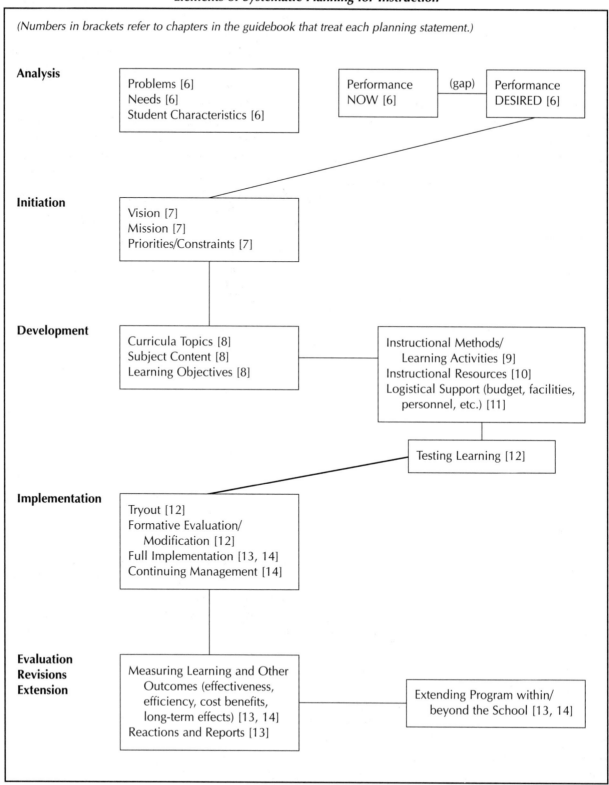

(Numbers in brackets refer to chapters in the guidebook that treat each planning statement.)

Analysis

Problems [6]
Needs [6]
Student Characteristics [6]

Performance NOW [6] — (gap) — Performance DESIRED [6]

Initiation

Vision [7]
Mission [7]
Priorities/Constraints [7]

Development

Curricula Topics [8]
Subject Content [8]
Learning Objectives [8]

Instructional Methods/
    Learning Activities [9]
Instructional Resources [10]
Logistical Support (budget, facilities,
    personnel, etc.) [11]

Testing Learning [12]

Implementation

Tryout [12]
Formative Evaluation/
    Modification [12]
Full Implementation [13, 14]
Continuing Management [14]

**Evaluation
Revisions
Extension**

Measuring Learning and Other
    Outcomes (effectiveness,
    efficiency, cost benefits,
    long-term effects) [13, 14]
Reactions and Reports [13]

Extending Program within/
    beyond the School [13, 14]

- A principal with vision, energy, and compassion.

- Teachers who are ready for change, enjoy the challenge of collaboration for the benefit of their students, and are supported in their efforts.

- Students who can be motivated toward success in learning, while acquiring basic skills and preparing for their roles in society.

- Services of an instructional designer to guide the planning process.

- Systemic changes in the instructional program, utilizing a systematic planning procedure.

- Available and emerging technological resources for improving and extending instruction and learning.

- Necessary funding, teacher-release time, and other recognized support as the program is developed and implemented.

- Endorsement by other school system personnel, including the superintendent and the school board.

As we proceed to examine the 16 components of systematic planning, you must not only keep in mind the above concepts of successful instructional transformation in a school, but also be prepared to implement and apply them, and help other interested or necessary persons to participate.

A POSTSCRIPT

As indicated previously, there have been some successful restructuring school efforts in recent years. A number of them apply many of the components of systemic change (to varying degrees) to be described here. The literature includes reports on the following:

- Accelerated School Program (Christine Finnan)

- Coalition of Essential Schools (Theodore Sizer)

- Effective Schools Process (Pamela Bullard and Barbara Taylor)

- New American Schools Design (Sam Stringfield)

- Project CHILD (Sarah Butzin)

- Schools Development Program (James Comer)

- Success for All (Robert Slavin)

See "References and Sources," Section M ("Successful Innovative School Projects"), on page 169 for information on these programs.

We are now prepared to proceed, in the following chapters of this guidebook, to develop answers to the 16 questions (pages 16–17) for systematically designing an innovative instructional program. ◆

NOTES

CHAPTER 4

An Overview of Components within the Systematic Design Plan

As indicated in the preface, the main audience for this guidebook is educators who want detailed information to guide them in transforming an instructional program. In addition, there are persons in the secondary audience category who may not be as concerned with all the details, but would like a summary view of what the process is about in terms of their interests and potential activities. This chapter provides a brief overview of the elements of systematic planning within the five phases introduced in Chapter 3. It may offer sufficient information for some readers, but you are also encouraged to scan the detailed explanations in the following chapters.

ANALYSIS PHASE

Before initiating a restructuring project, an examination of the present school program and its results should be made. This can reveal strengths as well as the need for improvements or changes. Attention should be given to both **schoolwide problems** and **student learning needs**. Data can be gathered from school records and reports, observations, questionnaires, and interviews with teachers, students, parents, and community representatives. The information obtained can provide the basis for initiating the new instructional program, and, after im-

plementation, can serve as the starting point for showing improvements and hopefully success.

See Chapter 6 for further analysis procedures.

INITIATION PHASE

Once the needs for a restructuring project have been clearly identified, a broad picture should be developed for what is to be accomplished in the new program. This image consists of two parts. The first is a **vision statement** in narrative form that describes the overall intent of what the program should become. The second is a list of the specific **mission goals,** including numerical standards to be achieved, that indicate how the vision would be attained. The vision and mission goals should relate to the Stage 3 principles, practices, and outcomes in the McBeath model of educational change (Figure 1, page 9). These two components establish the framework within which the program is to be developed.

Also at this early stage, recognition is given to priorities and constraints that may affect the project. Priorities include the time frame for implementing the program, and relationships between the new program and other school activities. Constraints may include limited funding and lack of necessary human or material resources available to the project.

Refer to Chapter 7 for further explanation of project initiation components.

Development phase

This phase serves as the core for the systematic planning process. Development includes a necessary educational structure consisting of seven related elements.

Curriculum topics

Curriculum topics should be selected according to mission goals and district requirements. They include **basic skills** in reading, writing, and mathematics; knowledge in other **academic subjects**; **interdisciplinary themes,** integrating content across subject areas such as history, literature, science, and math, that can provide a more realistic approach to learning for students; and practical **problem-based projects** that groups of students may research and investigate, leading to conclusions or solutions.

Subject content

Subject content relating to curriculum topics is identified. This includes **information** (facts, definitions, concepts, and principles), **procedures for skills** that must be performed, and **affective or interpersonal behaviors** such as attitudes, appreciations, and values students should acquire.

Learning objectives

As the results of selecting curriculum topics and subject content, learning objectives are written as the third element of this development phase. Objectives should specify the **competencies that students should attain,** using specific verbs such as "identify," "arrange," "compare," or "construct" to describe what is to be learned from the subject content. To this is added an accepted learning standard by which student accomplishment will be measured: for instance, "100 percent successful," "at least 8 out of 10 items correct," or "satisfactory completion within three minutes."

See Chapter 8 for full treatment of these first three developmental components.

Instructional methods and student activities

The curriculum components lead to decisions about instructional methods and student learning activities that are found within three groups: **teacher presents information** to students by lecturing, demonstrating, or showing media materials; **student self-directed and self-paced learning** through individual activities such as gathering and studying printed materials, using computer software, viewing media materials, conducting research, and preparing reports; and **group interactions** between teacher and students and among students by means of discussions, role playing, games, projects, and reports.

See Chapter 9 for full treatment of instructional methods and student learning activities.

Instructional resources

Instructional and learning activities can be supported by **conventional media** (texts, workbooks, objects, chalkboards, audio materials, photographs, and projected still and moving images), **instructional software, multimedia,** and the **Internet.** Resources should be carefully selected in terms of learning objectives and subject content to best fit the instructional method (presentation, self-paced learning, or group activity) in which they will be used. Also, students may prepare their own materials as part of project activities. In providing necessary resources, arranging for their use, and providing support services, the school needs to develop a technology plan.

See Chapter 10 for further treatment of instructional resources.

Logistics and program support

In this comprehensive planning process, a number of matters require consideration to provide instructional support and to overcome constraints identified as the project was initiated. These matters include **budget, facilities, materials** and **equipment** needs, and **personnel services** with necessary training to support the teachers. Time allocations, schedules for activities, and coordination with other school activities should also receive consideration.

See Chapter 11 for full details relating to logistical program support.

Testing learning

The evaluation component of the development phase relates directly to the **requirements stated in the learning objectives** prepared as the curriculum content is developed. Before the start of an instructional unit, each student's level of preparation can be determined by **pretesting**. This identifies any deficiencies that need to be overcome before beginning the new unit, and identifies students who may already have achieved some objectives and could skip ahead or engage in other studies.

As students proceed in a unit, each can determine how well he or she is learning by completing **self-check tests.** Then when instruction concludes, students are tested with **teacher-designated evaluations** that include written examinations, theme and project results, portfolios and reports, and cooperative work habits. The results not only can show content learning levels, but also can reveal creative talents, organizational skills, leadership abilities, and other higher intellectual and affective competencies acquired. If a student does not reach a required competency level, he or she can be given the opportunity to restudy and be retested to overcome any deficiencies specified by the objectives. Although all students may not always achieve all specified results, the great majority should reach a satisfactory learning level. Thus traditional grading (A, B, C, D, F) is eliminated in favor of assessing attained levels of *mastery learning* appropriate for each student. Some will acquire minimum competencies, and others should reach higher performance levels.

See Chapter 12 for information on all aspects of learning evaluation.

IMPLEMENTATION PHASE

Once a new or restructured instructional program has been developed, it should be tried out with a group of students, and the results should be evaluated in terms of the program goals and objectives. This is termed **formative evaluation**. It includes not only test results and other measurements, but also observations of students at work, their use of resources, personnel services provided, students' verbal reactions to the program, and suggestions from project staff participants (teachers, aides, parents, older students). This procedure can determine how students are progressing and identify any weakness in the instructional plan so that improvements can be made before full implementation takes place. Assurance of a satisfactory level of ongoing success can best be realized with this trial run and formative evaluation procedure. Once all operational aspects of the restructured program are functioning smoothly, **full-scale implementation** can take place.

For further information see pages 79–80 and Chapter 14.

FINAL PROGRAM EVALUATION PHASE

The results of a new or restructured program should be determined and reported each time it is implemented (usually yearly). This is the summative evaluation. It represents measures of accountability in terms of satisfying the needs initially identified and the specified mission goals prepared. These categories of measurement can be applied at this point: **effectiveness of student learning** (number of students accomplishing objectives at an acceptable level); **efficiency of the program** (ratio of teachers and staff to the number of students, facilities use, and time required by students to accomplish sets of objectives); **continuing program expenses** (including a cost-benefit analysis); **ongoing reactions to the program** by students, parents, and others involved; and **successful extension of the program** within the school or to other district schools.

See Chapter 13 for detailed information on summative evaluation procedures. ◆

CHAPTER 5

Preparing to Start the Transformation Process

▶ *How extensive will be the innovative project?*

▶ *Who will be on the planning team?*

As you prepare to examine and apply a systematic procedure for educational transformation, you should identify your own position relative to participating in this change process. Following the introduction of the McBeath model of educational change (Figure 1 on page 9), there were four important questions on page 10 you may have considered. Now you should further examine your interests. Which statement best represents your position?

1. I am somewhat motivated to explore new ideas for educational change.

2. I am curious about the approach the author takes to the change process.

3. I want to obtain some information about the proposed systematic planning process.

4. I have a real need to take action for change in our school.

Identify your particular focus. There are various reasons why teachers and others are interested in exploring this change process. Does one of the following fit your own interest or need?

- Modifying parts of regular class operation (such as moving toward more student self-directed learning, often with computer software).

- Redesigning a single course or a program.

- Restructuring the entire program within a school department.

- Transforming a total school program.

- Initiating an entirely new program or a completely new school operation.

Notice that this listing is sequenced from a least-involved restructuring effort to the most extensive and complex type—a total school transformation. Many people feel that the reform should be an immediate total change, involving all teachers in the school at one time. Experience has shown, however, that most often this procedure may not be feasible. Why?

- The complexity of the design and development procedure can best be managed as a gradual build-up and extension, starting from one or a few limited projects within a school.

- All teachers in the school may not be receptive and ready to engage in the change process at the same time.

- The potentially large amount of funding that may be required for resources and services for schoolwide change may not be available.

- There is always the need to get the support of stakeholders such as parents, school board members, and community representatives. After observing the development and results of a successful small project, stakeholders could be more receptive to a series of expanding projects that gradually lead to major restructuring of the entire school program.

Considering these challenges, a slower, carefully planned sequence of change efforts may be the best way to make school transformation successful. Initially, this should involve a team of interested and motivated teachers, and, in time, should extend to other teachers in the school, until after four to five years, the complete instructional program for the school is successfully transformed. This is the approach we will examine as we proceed.

COLLEAGUES AS CO-MEMBERS OF THE PLANNING TEAM

Hopefully, you are not the only person to be involved in an innovative project. While you may be the originator, organizer, or a key participant in a changed or new program, other individuals (teachers, administrators, parents, consultants, community representatives), who should be identified as needed or interested, can be motivated with a time commitment to participate in the project.

Also consider the knowledge and skills required for planning: program design, subject-matter and interdisciplinary topic competencies, nonconventional instructional methods, technology usage, learning evaluation techniques, and program result measurements. Select individuals with necessary, complementary, and special abilities to handle various responsibilities.

Do not expect everyone you approach about participation to be enthusiastic and willing to accept your invitation. Educators are often more comfortable with maintaining the status quo than with the discomfort of participating in change. (Don't we all behave this way to some degree with aspects of our own lives?) Therefore, it is necessary to identify those teachers who show a receptivity to change by their expressions of dissatisfaction or frustration with their present teaching and its results—someone who may say, "I'm not helping my students to learn successfully. There must be a better way to do this." Educators who express beliefs and practices typified by Stage 3 of the McBeath model (Figure 1 on page 9) would be predisposed toward change and more willing to participate.

As previously suggested, an effective approach to restructuring a school program is to start with a small group of concerned and motivated teachers, giving them administrative encouragement and support and the necessary professional planning guidance. Initiate the process gradually by examining the 16 questions on pages 16–17. Then, a small project can expand to include additional teachers in the school and other areas of curriculum and grade levels.

Consider names, scope of experience or personal interest, and what you might ask each person to do in the project. At this point, you may not be completely prepared to address this last concern because the needs for other persons' expertise or special services will better be recognized as we examine the components of the design plan in following chapters. (Also see the "Personnel Capabilities" portion of Chapter 11, starting on page 66.)

PERSONAL BEHAVIORS FOR PLANNING

Because there are no formulas or set procedures to follow, this design plan should be treated as a creative process. Therefore, for successful planning to take place, an environment should be established that supports positive group dynamics. Occasions for individuals to express their own thoughts and divergent viewpoints, while openly reacting to each other, are necessary. Such opportunities for introspective thinking, discussion, and response are needed in order to reach agreements or assess alternatives to be tried.

This interactive, continuous communication process can lead to shifts in beliefs, new awareness, and acceptance of fresh ideas. The experience itself can be very stimulating and thought provoking. Chapters 11 and 14 provide further treatment of personal behaviors.

READY TO PROCEED?

As stated, it is difficult to establish a specific recipe that directs the amount of consideration for the various planning elements that follow. While some level of attention should be given to each one, as we progress through the components of planning, decide for yourself what depth would be necessary for treatment of each component in your situation.

A side issue—the expression "educational transformation" is one of many terms used to define what is or can be taking place when a program is revised or a new one is developed. There are many labels being used to identify or describe the process. Common ones, combined with the words "educational" or "instructional," are:

- innovation
- redesign
- reengineering
- reformation
- restructuring
- transformation

You can select one or more terms that seem most suitable and descriptive for your purposes. Also, these expressions can be useful key search terms if you want to do library or Internet research to find out what other educators are doing or have written on the subject. ◆

CHAPTER 6

Analysis before Planning Starts

▶ *For what categories can data and personal reactions be gathered in a school's needs assessment?*

Be aware that any school reform that attempts to treat symptoms without identifying the real causes of any deficiencies will not be successful. With this in mind, initiate the project by examining the present school situation. Obviously, until you have a clear picture of the school's strengths and weaknesses, you cannot decide what program changes may be necessary.

Even though the present project may be limited to a few teachers and a portion of the total student body, consideration should be given not only to aspects of the total school operation but also to student learning needs and parent/community involvement. By examining school records and reports, making observations, developing and distributing questionnaires, and conducting interviews with teachers, students, parents, and community representatives, data and opinions can be obtained. Then the information should be objectively analyzed, with results summarized.

Any discrepancy between *what now is* and *what is desired or ought to be* would be the justification for initiating the improvement project. This information becomes the baseline against which the results of the new program can be judged as successful or not.

During this analysis period, it can be advantageous for members of the planning team to broaden their viewpoints by reading literature, visiting innovative school programs, attending conferences or workshops, and even consulting with experts about school needs and the transformation process. Such experiences and knowledge can better prepare teachers to initiate the change process, and help them become more aware of how they might proceed.

SCHOOL PROBLEMS

There may be broad needs within the school that are recognized as significant matters that affect morale and other aspects of the school program. From the information gathered and then analyzed, summary findings will reveal both strengths and weaknesses. Strengths in the school program are certainly commendable, and publicizing them can positively affect morale and other aspects of the school program. But it is the weaknesses that we need to identify and seek to correct.

Common educational problems that require attention may be grouped within the following three categories:

Schoolwide concerns

- Violence and vandalism in the school disrupt learning.

- Student absenteeism, dropout rates, or discipline problems are excessive.

- Many teachers express dissatisfaction with their teaching and their success rates with students.

Individual student problems

- Student grades on standardized or state-level tests are below acceptable levels.

- Too many students are either left back in their grades each year or receive unmerited social promotion.

- A wide achievement difference exists between advantaged and disadvantaged students.

- Too many students show boredom or even negative attitudes toward school and learning.

Community concerns

- Parents show little interest in the school, other than in their own child's accomplishments or deficiencies.

- The general reputation of the school in the community is low.

- Community representatives, especially business interests, are dissatisfied with the vocational preparation and interpersonal skills of school graduates.

Which of these problems are important to you? There certainly could be other deficiencies that require attention in the school. It may be necessary for you to be observant, do some careful thinking, have conversations with colleagues, read local statistics and reports, or otherwise consider the educational situation that indicates that a program needs to be transformed.

STUDENT LEARNING NEEDS AND CHARACTERISTICS

Every business today, whether in manufacturing, retail, or services, assesses the needs of its customers in order to best serve them. This concern certainly contributes to monetary profits. Disregarding the profit motive, the customer-service mentality must also be

present in education. A key concept on the Stage 3 level of the McBeath model of educational change (Figure 1 on page 9) is "the teacher doing things *with* students." As we know, this causes a different approach to teaching than in the "doing things *to*" and "*for*" practices of Stages 1 and 2. This approach requires that you have a clear understanding of the overall nature of the student group, including their emotional, physical, and psychological characteristics, their family and neighborhood relations, and detailed personal and academic information about each student.

Learning styles

It is increasingly being recognized that students' learning styles do have an important bearing on their success in learning. Learning styles are indicators of how individual students prefer to gather and process information. The preferences involve using choices of kinesthetic, visual, auditory, verbal, or combinations of these methods for experiencing learning.

Identifying learning styles used by individual students is often both difficult and uncertain within any clear categories. Where feasible, when given more than a single instructional method and a variety of different resources to accomplish a set of objectives, each student can find a most successful method for learning. For example, verbal presentation and reading textual material could be supplemented with more visual materials, with the possible manipulation of objects, and with group participation activities. Thus a student would have the opportunity to study and learn in more than one way, and can choose a way that would be most comfortable for him or her. It is in part because of different learning styles that we will give detailed attention to the various patterns of instruction and learning in Chapter 9.

For further information on learning styles, see "References and Sources," Section D, page 166.

Gathering data

Some of the data you would want to acquire about each student include:

- Scores on intelligence tests and competencies in the basic subjects of reading, writing, and mathematics.

- Grade point average, letter grades, or other evaluations in previous academic courses.

- Appraisals of the student's motivation, attitudes, expectations and vocational aspirations, special talents, and sensory learning styles.

- School behavior activities, including attendance, discipline problems, and at-risk behaviors.

- To the degree possible, sociological information and cultural characteristics about each student's family situation (income, employment, parents' education), peer influences, and out-of-school experiences.

Evidence from the above factors can help a teacher determine if the student is ready to accept more freedom and would profit from the Stage 3 instructional concept of a teacher "doing things *with* students." Many students no doubt will still be dependent on the teacher to "doing things *to*" them, and will need to be nurtured to advance to responsibilities inherent in the "doing things *with*" level.

Consider using the services of a testing specialist to select or develop data-gathering instruments and to interpret results. (For example, useful suggestions on the issue of handling school dropouts are treated in Murphy and Schiller, page 178; see "References and Sources," Section B, page 165.)

Anticipated learning results

A guiding principle for the success of this systematic planning process is that the great majority of students (up to 95 percent) can accomplish what is required of them if each individual:

- is motivated to learn,

- has suitable academic preparation,

- receives carefully designed instruction with content that is meaningful,

- participates actively in assigned or selected activities, and

- has sufficient time to complete the learning with opportunities to self-test and review as necessary.

(This principle, with the above supporting actions, is derived from Bloom, *Human Characteristics*

and School Learning, in "References and Sources," Section D, page 166.)

The increasing interest in results of standardized testing in all grades is an effort to attain levels of satisfactory competencies by students. In California, there is a recommendation by an Advisory Committee to the State Superintendent of Public Instruction that "in the next 10 years, 90 [percent] of students should perform at or above their grade level" (reported in *California Curriculum News Report*, March 1998, Hayward, CA: Alameda County Office of Education, page 3). See further discussion of standardized testing on pages 80–81 of this guidebook.

The foregoing results anticipated by both Bloom and the California Advisory Committee bring again to attention the slogan on page 3: *It's a new plan for instruction we need, my friends!* Note that Bloom, in his list of requirements leading to the 95 percent student accomplishment level, includes the expression, "receives carefully designed instruction." Guiding you to do this is a main goal of this guidebook.

To best accomplish this principle, the planning team needs to find out as much as possible about the students, and then use this information as each phase of instruction is planned and implemented. When we examine "Phases in Evaluation of Learning" in Chapter 12, one topic is pretesting students to assess their preparation for studying a subject. The results can help teachers to set objectives and subject-content levels, and to plan for a range of instruction, including remedial, preparatory, and advanced learning activities.

PARENT AND COMMUNITY INVOLVEMENT WITH THE SCHOOL

The holistic approach to educational reform recommended here requires recognition of the many elements that can contribute to or influence an educational program. In today's society, a school cannot operate in isolation from its community. It must be integrated through a cooperative and coordinated relationship with other community agencies and functions. (Recall the school-community description in the introductory visionary situation by P. M. Senge on page xvii.) Therefore, one consideration early in the planning process is to decide what relationship those involved in a new program will have with parents and community organizations. Consider the following questions:

- What is the nature of the community served by the school?

- Will the school attempt to educate severely handicapped, emotionally disturbed, or violent children?

- Will the school attempt to deal with children's health, family, nutrition, and economic problems, as well as with usual educational issues?

- Can the school coordinate with local law enforcement and their school resource officers in working on gangs, drug and alcohol use, child abuse and molestation, teen pregnancy, or crime and violence?

- How can the school and its students benefit from coordination with business concerns and other community organizations?

- In turn, how can the organizations profit from school contacts?

(Questions adapted from Salisbury, page 26; see "References and Sources," Section B, page 166.)

The answers to these questions are inextricably linked and certainly can broaden the responsibilities of the school beyond the academic growth and development of individual students. Without some degree of community coordination, control and even success with troubled or troublesome students could be seriously hampered, which could in turn negatively influence other students and disrupt normal school functions. While treatment of potential extracurricular functions for a school is beyond the scope of this guidebook, you should give this matter careful consideration. (Possibly consider including school-sponsored activities before and/or after normal school hours, such as special tutoring, apprenticeship work, field trips, and physical fitness training.) Consult with other knowledgeable persons as planning proceeds. We will treat direct curricula matters that require involvement with and support from community groups and individuals as we develop planning.

For an illustration of a neighborhood school that has been transformed into a "caring community," see "It Takes a School" in the June 3, 1996, issue of *Time* magazine (page 36). On the other end of the education scale, check the description of the Delancey Street program in San Francisco (reported in the *San Francisco Examiner* Sunday magazine section, October 20, 1996)—it is one of the world's most successful programs for hard-core criminal rehabilitation after release from prison. Participants learn to read, attain high school equivalency, acquire job skills, start a personal bank account, and through many community experiences prepare themselves for a new life. Ten thousand "graduates" of the Delancey Street program have started successful lives through it. This is a good example of how an organization takes into account the many personal, societal, and economic influences that must be faced, and, in practical ways, controls them for the benefits of its "students." It can offer ideas for any school's new program.

Furthermore, in the past, schools have been thought of as the only places in which education can take place. But every community possesses human, physical, and financial resources that could be available to improve and extend a school's program. The utilization of these resources occurs when community features are brought into the school and when students participate in the community. (See Otterbourg, *A Business Guide to Support Employee and Family Involvement in Education,* in "References and Sources," Section L, page 169.)

As part of the needs assessment survey during this analysis phase, carefully formulated questions can gather such information as the following:

- Parent participation or interest in school activities (attending meetings, consulting with teachers, voluntary services, assisting child with homework, other school interests).

- Features of the community neighborhood being served, including public services such as law enforcement, athletics, and commercial interests.

- Potential community involvement with the school (agency and organizational activities, corporate cooperation, employee volunteerism, technical services available, financial assistance, student visitations).

See page 132 in Appendix B for an example of attitudinal questions for parents as a new program is considered.

SPECIFYING NEEDS

As indicated, the needs should reflect the problems. Recognize needs that are entirely new, those that are not presently being served, and those not presently at an adequate level of accomplishment. When stating a need, describe the problem as specifically as possible. For example:

- "Present student dropout rate from our school is 12 percent."

- "Reading levels average three grades below normal."

- "Our students rate in the lowest 25th percentile on standardized math examinations."

- "More than 50 percent of our teachers feel that the school should do a better job with students."

- "While our high school best prepares students for postsecondary education, significantly less is being done for students who plan to enter vocations from high school."

- "Only 15 percent of parents attend open-house meetings."

- "We have almost no contact with the business community."

For your own situation, determine the identified school and student needs. The descriptions of shortcomings will become important statements because, after you design and implement the new program, you will come back to these problems and the needs list to decide how well each problem is being overcome, and what further changes in the new education program may be necessary to better meet the school's needs. ◆

CHAPTER 7

Initial Planning

▶ *How can planning start to seek answers to the needs identified?*

A VISION STATEMENT

Follow the identification of the problems to be overcome and needs to be served by deciding on a vision that describes the desired future you and others on the planning team want to attain. This is a statement of the philosophy and overall intent of what the school and its program should become. It leads to systematic instructional reform.

Each participating individual—teacher, administrator, parent, and community member—should have the opportunity to both contribute to and react to the vision statement. Thus it becomes a shared vision. If you have accepted McBeath's three-stage model of educational change presented in Figure 1 on page 9, then the principles, practices, and outcomes for Stage 3 should become a reference for your vision, and lead to the operational aspects of your new program. An example of a vision statement for a middle school is shown at right. Another vision statement example can be found in Appendix A on page 102.

Now to your situation. Again, review the assessment of problems and needs you have already formulated. Then ask the question, "With respect to these recognized problems and needs and our beliefs and desires, what do we broadly want to happen in this school (program)?" You may want to formulate an answer yourself and then have it reviewed by the planning team, colleagues, and other interested persons. Or, you may decide to involve them directly in developing the statement.

> Each student, from any cultural background, can learn and succeed, each to his or her highest potential level. It is the role of our school, with involvement of parents and community representatives, to guide each student, in terms of his or her learning style, to reach his or her potential by means of a variety of successful learning experiences with the leadership of a dedicated and knowledgeable faculty.

Example of a vision statement for a middle school

MISSION GOALS

Follow the vision statement by answering this question: "What must happen in the school to accomplish this vision?" The answers to this question become a series of goals as the school's specific mission. They spell out how to attain the vision with detailed outcomes. The goals relate to the needs identified in Chapter 6. An example of mission goals for the above vision statement is provided on page 36. Another example appears in Appendix A on page 102.

Notice that some of the goals contain numerical standards that can be measured for accomplishment as program implementation proceeds. Successive gains should be realized, possibly along a timeline, until the program is fully implemented (probably within three to four years). Other goals are more attitudinal, requiring activities or subjective judgments to determine achievement. Then, during both formative evaluation (pages 79–80 and 151–152) and summative evaluation (see Chapter 13), measurements can determine the degree to which these goals are being accomplished.

The school will offer a strong support system for student learning so the following goals can be accomplished:

- Student dropout rate will decline to below 4 percent within three years.

- Standardized scores and competencies for students in basic knowledge and communication skills in reading, writing, speaking, and listening will increase 20 percent per year to surpass grade-level norms within three years.

- Ninety percent of our students will acquire understandings and gain competencies in language arts, mathematics, the sciences, and the social studies, at least to the levels specified for the national America 2000 agenda, within three years.

- At least 90 percent of our students will show accomplishments on at least a satisfactory level for all curriculum topics beyond basic skills and understandings stated above.

- Each student will be able to locate and to process information; then apply and use it in creative, realistic ways for critical thinking and problem solving.

- Each student will develop skills to be both a self-directed learner and a cooperative member of activity-oriented study groups.

- Each student will become competent and comfortable in using technological resources for learning.

- Each student will recognize and respect the moral and democratic principles essential to American society.

- Each student will be prepared to become a responsible member of a family and active in the local community.

- Each student will show sensitivity to individuals with cultural differences.

- Each student will become aware of the growing global interdependence among nations.

- All students will start to develop a perspective on responsibilities and opportunities relating to future employment.

- There will be practical, realistic steps taken by the school to encourage and support parental participation, resulting in at least 60 percent parental involvement within three years.

- There will be active involvement of community individuals and groups in the school's educational program.

Example of mission goals

PRIORITIES AND CONSTRAINTS

While you are engaging in the intellectual activities of preparing a vision statement and deciding on mission goals, it also is necessary to face other essential practical issues. They can have a direct bearing on how you carry through the program development and then its implementation. Consider the following questions:

- How will this program relate to other activities within the school or district? (relationships)

- By what date must or should the program be ready for use? (time frame)

- What funds will be available for planning and development, or does a special grant have to be obtained? (monetary resources)

- What person(s) will be available for planning and development? (planning team, consultants)

- What other support services will be available for program development? (logistics, including personnel services, facilities, and schedules)

- What will be the anticipated level of administrative, colleague, parental, and community support for the project? (support range)

Other additional questions may be important to you. Add them to this list. Also, realize that further logistical matters certainly will arise and have to be recognized and acted upon as you proceed. ◆

CHAPTER 8

Curriculum Topics, Subject Content, and Learning Objectives

▶ *How can curriculum topics be chosen?*

▶ *How is subject content selected for topics and related to objectives?*

▶ *Why are learning objectives important in an instructional program?*

▶ *To what four types of learning should the objectives relate?*

▶ *What comprises a learning objective, and how are the components stated?*

▶ *What are the benefits of pretesting students on a topic to be studied?*

We are at a place in our planning with which teachers should feel most comfortable—the topics and subject matter for their grade level or academic area. But be alert to a reality in present educational practices. Subject textbooks and accompanying teacher's guides have enormous influence over classroom instruction. It may take real effort to reexamine and decide on subject topics and content from fresh Stage 3 viewpoints according to the McBeath model (Figure 1 on page 9).

CURRICULUM TOPICS

Based on the mission goals and the characteristics of the students, these questions should be asked:

- What curriculum subjects and content should every student achieve mastery of? (basic skills)

- Should topics be organized for separate subject discipline treatment, or, when feasible, across subjects as interdisciplinary themes?

- How can other topics or issues be selected for group and individual projects?

Some of the answers to these questions may be dictated by state or district requirements. But even so, how the required content is organized and taught are usually school-level decisions. (For a useful explanation of ways to restructure curriculum content in major subject areas, see Chapter 4 in Murphy and

Schiller, listed in "References and Sources," Section B, page 165.)

Basic skills

Skills in reading, writing, and arithmetic, especially in lower grades, may continue to be taught as separate subject areas. Recognition of individual student cultural uniqueness, cognitive development, and individual learning styles may best be served through widely accepted instructional methods followed with hands-on drill-and-practice activities using a variety of resources. Then, as skills are developed, they would be applied while students study other subject areas within the following curriculum settings.

Subject disciplines

Although many curriculum topics could be treated within interdisciplinary themes to be considered next, to adequately cover required curricula in literature, social studies, mathematics, and science, separate courses may continue to be scheduled. But the manner of teaching subject topics can shift significantly. Refer to the methods and activity patterns in Chapter 9 for suggested ways to do this. Strive to relate content of subject topics to higher levels of learning, as described for sequencing objectives on page 45. This treatment may apply also to health, foreign languages, vocational, and elective courses.

Interdisciplinary themes

By integrating content across subject areas that treat a theme or an issue, a more realistic approach to learning can take place. Do not science and math topics frequently relate? Cannot history, science, and literature be correlated? Interdisciplinary themes allow more challenging learning, along with practical applications of basic skills, to be accomplished. A good explanation of ways to select and organize interdisciplinary curricula can be found in Erickson and in Roberts and Kellough (see "References and Sources," Section F, page 166). They include useful procedures for designing integrated teaching units. Also, sample themes are described with recommendations of how students can be involved in planning units, and otherwise participate actively in what they will study. Sounds sensible and useful, right? This relates directly to "doing things *with* students," from Stage 3 in the McBeath model (Figure 1 on page 9).

Refer to pages 111–113 in Appendix A for further developmental suggestions on interdisciplinary themes. Also, see Chapter 26 for an example of how a conventional topic relating to subject areas can be integrated into an interdisciplinary theme.

Problem-based projects

A third way to handle and eventually extend curricula, while providing for learning in groups or by individuals, is to assign or allow students to choose meaningful problems or issues of interest to research and investigate, leading to conclusions or solutions. While this approach is out of the ordinary in terms of handling conventional curriculum content, a project can include applications of many basic skills and subject concepts while providing important learning experiences for students. These applications may include planning, engaging in exploration and analysis, doing research, interacting together verbally, making decisions, locating and organizing information, reaching conclusions, reporting results, and developing important interpersonal group skills.

Some general project questions that middle school and high school students might investigate are:

- What do people eat for lunch, and how nutritious is it?

- How can we judge the values offered by commercial entertainment (television, movies, computer games, the Internet)?

- What kinds of new vocations are becoming available in our community?

- Can we trace the development of our community in terms of ethnic diversity, transportation, and business growth?

Judge the suitability of a problem-based project with these criteria:

- Is the project useful and practical, with broad meaningful applications?

- Will it be of interest to students?

- How will the learning relate to curricula topics and subject concepts or principles?

- Is a variety of necessary resources, including knowledgeable persons, available?

- Is it acceptable to and manageable by the teachers in terms of their knowledge and experiences?

- Can it be implemented by students in a reasonable amount of time?

Refer to Chapter 19, starting on page 115 in Appendix A, for suggestions relative to developing problem-based projects, and also to Chapter 28, starting on page 153 in Appendix B, for how such a project can be implemented with students.

As you proceed with your planning, decide how to structure the content in the new instructional program. Be creative. Gradually allow students to select and guide some of their own learning. Try to lay out a plan that is more "real world" than the artificial subject divisions treated in many curriculum guides. Consider community-based problems or recent news-related projects that require multisubject treatments. This approach can stimulate students to become more interested and active through participation in meaningful learning experiences. Be sure to recognize special interests and abilities of teachers who will direct the instruction.

Finally, it may be helpful to glance ahead to the topics addressed in Chapter 9, "Instructional Methods and Learning Activities," and Chapter 10, "Instructional Resources." You may wish to keep them in mind, as they can influence how you select topics, structure curriculum content, and specify objectives.

SUBJECT CONTENT

Once a curriculum topic or theme has been specified, then the supporting content should be outlined. Subject content can be specified in four domains of learning, or overlapped among them.

Cognitive domain—information or knowledge, thinking, and other intellectual aspects of learning. Included in the cognitive domain are:

- names, symbols, labels, places

- definitions

- descriptions of objects and events

- other facts and terms essential to a topic

- concepts as single terms or statements that relate facts, objects, or events having common features that can lead to simple inferences

- principles, laws, or rules that are broad generalizations of the relationship between two or more concepts; the application of a principle can become a problem-solving activity, can establish causal connections, or result in predictions

Psychomotor domain—information and kinesthetic activity for a physical skill or a task requiring the use and coordination of skeletal muscles. Included in the psychomotor domain are:

- necessary subject content (forms of cognitive learning as above), probably before the skill is performed (see *learning to use a tool*, below)

- procedural steps for performing the process or task

- attention to safety factors

- higher-level skills, including more sophisticated techniques, troubleshooting, and applications of the process

Affective domain—attitudes, appreciations, beliefs, values, and other emotional expressions.

Interpersonal domain—verbal or nonverbal skills for interacting with other people. The affective and interpersonal domains are related; thus they are often considered together as a single behavioral category for learning. Attitudinal development often precedes successful learning in the other domains because it may be necessary to motivate and interest students (affective domain behaviors) to want to learn subject content before instruction can be successful.

Interrelation of domains

A single concept can involve learning in more than a single domain. For example, *learning to use a tool* requires:

- an understanding of uses for the tool (cognitive)

- names of parts and their functions (cognitive)

- procedure for using the tool (psychomotor)

- safety requirements (may include cognitive, psychomotor, and affective)

- manner of handling the tool (psychomotor and affective)

- manipulating the tool for actual uses (cognitive, psychomotor, and affective)

Subject content becomes a means, not an end, for learning. Acquisition of subject matter, while important, should not be through rote memorization. Content is best understood and applied in real-life activities, including those that develop problem-solving skills and other higher-level thinking skills such as comprehension, analysis, synthesis, and evaluation. Refer to the five levels of the cognitive domain above Level 1 (the knowledge or recall level) in Figure 3 on page 44. As we will see, these terms are used when preparing learning objectives. For fresh approaches to the organization and treatment of subject content, see Harless (Chapters 6 and 7) and Kemp et al. (Chapter 7), listed in "References and Sources," Section E, page 166.

LEARNING OBJECTIVES

Learning objectives specify the required outcomes for students when studying curriculum topics or themes and engaging in projects. They are usually derived from subject content. Such terms as "instructional objectives," "behavioral objectives," or even "performance objectives" may be used, but the expression "learning objectives" is used here because objectives are designed and worded to direct student learning.

When students are informed of the objectives to be attained, they become aware of what they are to learn, and the skills, attitudes, and relationships they are to develop. Here are other advantages for preparing learning objectives:

- Specifying objectives allows teachers to recognize and judge the need for and value of what they will be teaching.

- Objectives guide teachers in planning instruction, selecting sequence of content, and choosing learning activities.

- Objectives provide the requirements for devising tests and other evaluation methods for determining learning accomplishments.

- Objectives can help students organize their study time and efforts to learn.

- Ultimately, the success of an instructional program, and the teacher's accountability, are based on student accomplishment of learning objectives.

The learning objective is one component of systematic planning that many teachers are aware of, but need assistance to handle competently, especially regarding the role of students in identifying their objectives and in recognizing the benefits they can derive from them.

Learning objective domains

As with subject content, objectives for learning can be grouped into the four major domains of learning. (See "References and Sources," Section G, page 167.)

- Cognitive domain—naming, solving, organizing, and predicting (Bloom; Martin and Briggs)

- Psychomotor domain—performing, manipulating, using, and constructing (Harrow)

- Affective domain—caring, conserving, supporting, and respecting (Krathwohl et al.; Martin and Briggs)

- Interpersonal domain—cooperating, assisting others, taking leadership, and sharing responsibilities within a team (Martin and Briggs)

Behaviors in the affective and interpersonal domains are difficult to identify, let alone to specify as content and as learning objectives, then to measure for learning accomplishment. Attitudes can be recognized only indirectly from secondary clues. For example, behaviors for the affective learning objective "Demonstrate habits of good nutrition" could be indicated by:

- acquiring information about foods of high nutritional value (after satisfying objectives that identify nutritional components of foods)

- voluntarily reading books and articles, or otherwise acquiring information that describes good nutritional practices

- talking with and advising other students about the value of nutritious foods

- selecting lunch and snack items having good nutritional value

An example from the interpersonal domain is the learning objective, "Exhibit a sensitivity toward various ethnic groups." The related behaviors that indicate successful accomplishment of this objective can be recognized from clues such as:

- showing an interest and concern for individuals of other ethnic cultures

- exhibiting polite and courteous behavior toward such persons

- having patience and understanding during disputes with such individuals

- offering help when such an individual needs assistance

By observing or otherwise judging behaviors and actions like the two sets above, a decision can be made about the degree to which an affective or interpersonal objective has been achieved.

Preparing objectives

Remember, a learning objective is a precise statement of observable and measurable student behavior. It answers the question, "What should the student learn relative to the subject content, skill, or behavior required for this topic?" Educators may shy away from stating precise learning objectives because formulating them demands much thought and effort. Teaching is often based on broad generalizations, leaving it up to the students to interpret what is actually meant and what they are required to learn. Each objective should be unambiguous. It must communicate exactly the same thing to all students and also to other teachers. The following is a procedure for carefully stating learning objectives.

Start with two essential parts:

1. An **action verb** that describes the required learning, as shown with each domain above

(For help in selecting verbs for use in learning objectives, refer to Figures 3, 4, and 5 on page 44.) Note that certain verbs or expressions, such as "master," "understand," "learn about," and "become familiar with," are **not** acceptable for use in learning objectives. While these words are appropriate for broad academic standards or goal statements, they are *not specific* enough to indicate required measurable learning.

2. The **subject reference** that describes the content to be treated, such as:

- Name **the parts of speech used in a sentence.**

- Operate **a videocassette recorder.**

- Offer **to assist other students.**

In addition, an objective may include one or two optional parts:

3. A **performance standard** that indicates the minimum acceptable accomplishment in measurable terms, such as:

- in proper order

- at least 8 out of 10, or at an accuracy level of 80 percent

- with an accuracy of two inches

- within three minutes

- meeting the criteria established by the class or group

There are two accepted alternatives for interpretation of a performance standard in an objective. First, performance results could be assessed as acceptable on either of two levels: on a satisfactory or minimally acceptable level (as in the examples above), or on a superior or excellent accomplishment level (100 percent, appreciably less than the required three minutes, and so forth). Second, when an objective does not include a performance standard, the assumption should be made that only 100 percent accomplishment, in terms of the requirement specified by the verb, is acceptable.

(Continued on page 45)

FIGURE 3
Verbs for Objectives in the Cognitive Domain

(In Stage 3 of the McBeath model of educational change [Figure 1 on page 9], we recognize the need for learning above Level 1: rote learning and recall of information.)

Level 1: Knowledge		Level 2: Comprehension		Level 3: Application	
Recall information		*Interpret information in one's own words*		*Use knowledge or generalization in a new situation*	
arrange	name	classify	locate	apply	operate
define	order	describe	recognize	choose	practice
duplicate	recall	discuss	report	demonstrate	prepare
label	recognize	explain	restate	dramatize	schedule
list	relate	express	review	employ	sketch
match	repeat	identify	select	illustrate	solve
memorize	reproduce	indicate	translate	interpret	use
Level 4: Analysis		**Level 5: Synthesis**		**Level 6: Evaluation**	
Break down knowledge into parts and show relationships among parts		*Bring together parts of knowledge to form a whole and build new relationships among parts*		*Make judgments on the basis of given criteria*	
analyze	differentiate	arrange	organize	appraise	evaluate
appraise	discriminate	assemble	plan	argue	judge
calculate	distinguish	collect	prepare	assess	predict
categorize	examine	compose	propose	attack	rate
compare	experiment	construct	set up	choose	score
contrast	inventory	design	synthesize	compare	select
criticize	question	formulate	write	defend	support
diagram	test	manage		estimate	value

Depending on meaning and usage, some verbs may apply to more than one level.

FIGURE 4
Verbs for Objectives in the Psychomotor Domain

adjust	drill	perform
analyze	form	pour
assemble	grasp	roll
balance	hit	run
build	lift	set
calibrate	locate	sketch
design	mix	step
draw	obtain	throw

FIGURE 5
Verbs for Objectives in the Affective and Interpersonal Domains

acclaim	cooperate	offer
agree	defend	participate in
argue	disagree	praise
assume responsibility	dispute	resist
attempt	engage in	respect
avoid	help	share
be attentive to	join	support
challenge	obey	volunteer

4. Any **conditions** under which the learning would take place:

- based on the assigned readings

- using the United States map

- with the ABC software program

By applying these four steps you can write unambiguous objectives that directly specify learning outcomes. Here are two important points:

1. Avoid objectives that require a specific instructional event, such as "View the video on watercolor techniques." This is *an activity* that may help a student accomplish a learning objective. It is *not* an objective itself.

2. Do not include multiple sequential learning steps in one objective, like this: "*Identify* what five significant writers predict about the future, and *explain* how they arrived at their opinions." It is better for students' understanding and sequential learning to write separate, related objectives like these:

   a. After choosing one social or scientific area, predict in detail how it may be changed by the year 2010.

   b. Assess the possible effects of the change upon you as an individual.

Academic standards and objectives

The subject-content standards that have become important to educators are closely related to learning objectives. These standards can be considered as broad major purposes to be achieved. For example, an eighth-grade standard in California contains this statement:

> *A student should develop an understanding of the symbolic language of mathematics and the sciences.*

As you will recall from page 43, the expression "develop an understanding" is not appropriate for a measurable learning objective. As an overall starting point for the topic, though, it may be acceptable. Related to it should be specific measurable objectives that indicate precisely what students are to learn in order to reach the goal indicated by the standard. The learning objectives for the above standard would include:

> - Solve equations and inequities involving absolute values.
>
> - Graph a linear equation.
>
> - Explain the difference between inductive and deductive reasoning.

Review the standards in your subject fields, and develop specific, measurable learning objectives that represent what must be learned to accomplish the standard.

Sequencing objectives

Learning about a topic usually starts with simple facts, which are then used to build understandings and higher-order intellectual skills, or more complex procedural skills. Figure 3 illustrates the six levels in the cognitive domain: *knowledge, comprehension, application, analysis, synthesis,* and *evaluation*). Note the verbs listed for accomplishing the principle on each level. For any curriculum topic, learning objectives should be sequenced on progressively higher levels (not necessarily treating all six levels). Here is an example:

> **Topic:**
> "Historical Conflict in the 20th Century"
>
> **Knowledge:** Define the term "Cold War."
>
> **Comprehension:** Locate five battlefronts on which the Cold War was fought.
>
> **Application:** Illustrate through examples the pace of the development of the Cold War from 1946 to 1968.
>
> **Synthesis:** Organize information that summarizes the nature and extent of the Russia-China split.
>
> **Evaluation:** Assess the evidence presented for and against the "thaw" in the Cold War.

Objectives can also relate to two broad organizational levels:

- **Major objectives** that specify the *principal learning outcome* for each topic; these may be derived from the aforementioned subject standard

- **Enabling objectives** that detail, often sequentially, the subject matter, skills, and other behavioral components that must be learned as part of the major objective (for example, *names, definitions, descriptions, concepts,* and *principles*)

Here's an example on a science topic (*Using Solar Energy*):

Major: When provided with the essential parts, assemble and operate a solar collector as judged satisfactory on a checklist.

Enabling:

- Explain how four scientific principles are applied for creating heat in a solar collector. (application)

- Identify four parts of a solar collector. (knowledge)

- Describe functions of each part. (comprehension)

- Construct a solar collector. (psychomotor and application)

Writing objectives is a developmental activity that may require changes, refinements, and additions as teaching/learning activities and evaluation methods are decided upon. For more detailed information and guidance on preparing objectives, see "References and Sources," Section G, page 167.

Shown at right is an example of an interdisciplinary theme with the subject-content outline and learning objectives. (See page 146 in Appendix B for another example of objectives for an interdisciplinary theme, and see Figure 7 on page 74.)

Prior to or at the start of a new topic, theme, or project, plan to inform students of the learning objectives for which they'll be responsible, or assist them in developing ones to accomplish themselves. ◆

The Industrial Revolution
(partial development)

Subject Content

A. Developments in Industry
   1. Textiles
   2. Blast furnace and forge
   3. Pottery

B. Developments of Power
   1. Water wheel
   2. Steam engine

C. Developments in Transportation
   1. Roads and canals
   2. Bridges
   3. Steam locomotives and railroads
   4. Steamboats

D. Effects on British Society
   1. Daily life
   2. Home to factory work
   3. Industrial cities
   4. Living costs and wages
   5. Owners' relationships to workers

Learning Objectives

Major: Relate the progress made during the Industrial Revolution to the contributions that followed in Europe.

Enabling:

- Describe the conditions of life in England early in the 18th Century. (social studies)

- Name six inventions that were created during the Industrial Revolution. (science)

- State five fundamental scientific principles applied to the inventions. (science)

- Compare costs of living and wages during the Industrial Revolution with comparable costs and wages today. (math)

- Summarize the contributions of two leaders or inventors during the Industrial Revolution. (literature)

- Describe how the developments during the 18th Century influenced the times that have followed. (writing)

CHAPTER 9

Instructional Methods and Learning Activities

▶ *What are three patterns of instruction and learning within which all methods can be placed?*

▶ *What methods are appropriate within each pattern?*

▶ *How can you decide on the best methods to use for accomplishing sets of learning objectives?*

There can be many paths to learning. Let us review the patterns of teaching and learning activities with which teachers are generally familiar.

- A **teacher presents information** to a class of students through lecturing, talking informally, writing on the chalkboard, demonstrating, or using media materials.

- **Students work individually, each self-directed at his or her own pace** by reading, completing activities, solving problems, working in a laboratory, viewing media materials, using computer-based resources, preparing reports, and checking his or her own level of learning.

- **Interaction between the teacher and students and among students** takes place by means of question-and-answer sessions, discussion, small-group activities, and project work in school or the community.

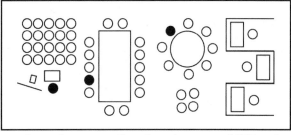

Presentation *Group Interactions* *Self-Directed*

These three patterns—presentation to a class, self-directed or individualized learning, and teacher-students or student-student interactions—are the categories within which all methods of instruction and learning can be placed. Each pattern has certain features and activities as described on the following pages. The choice of instructional method and student activities should depend on the nature of the subject content and learning objectives, along with the methods you prefer to use or have identified as most suitable for your students. Consider the range of student learning styles introduced on page 30. The questions listed on pages 36–37 can assist a planning team in making selections.

PRESENTATION PATTERN

In this pattern, the student is usually confined to passive learning: listening and watching, possibly taking notes, with little or no opportunity for interchange of ideas, unless questions or discussion are parts of the teacher's procedure. Consider the following situations and times in which a presentation can be of value:

- As an introduction, overview, or orientation to a new topic or theme.

- To motivate students by creating interest in the topic or theme, often by viewing a video, a multimedia presentation, or having a meaningful experience such as on a field trip.

- To present basic or essential background information in order to prepare students most efficiently for group or individual activities.

- To provide a one-time guest speaker.

- To provide a video or other visual program that can conveniently present information to the entire class at the same time.

- To offer a presentation or aspects of a course through electronic distance learning as an effective and efficient teaching method, often combined with computer networking or other group and individual activities.

- To provide opportunities for students to make presentations as reports to the whole class.

- As a review or summary when study of a topic is concluding.

There are advantages and disadvantages to the presentation pattern. For efficiency, large numbers of students can be provided with information at one time; and a presentation can be adaptable, allowing modification as necessary. While this pattern may seem to save time because more content can be presented in a given period than by other patterns, there are limitations. One common drawback is student passivity. Another is the generally made assumption that all students are acquiring the same understandings at the same level of comprehension at the same time. We know this doesn't happen. There may not be opportunities for feedback from learners on misunderstandings and learning difficulties. The result is that some students may acquire an incomplete or incorrect understanding of the content.

SELF-DIRECTED LEARNING

Research on student learning indicates the need to recognize that:

- Every student is not "ready" to study a topic at the same time, regardless of a teacher's efforts to prepare students and create interest.

- Students have different levels of preparation for studying a topic or a theme, some requiring preparatory activities to overcome learning deficiencies.

- Students may progress through a unit of study at various rates, some requiring more time, more examples, or opportunities to review what they specifically need to learn.

- Students have differing ability levels, some requiring more guidance, practice, and feedback on progress.

- Because students have different learning styles, more than a single instructional method would be appropriate, with various resources being available for student use.

Each of the above factors supports the applications of self-directed learning. In this case, individual students receive information, respond to it, and interact with it. They can be guided to "learn how to learn" and to develop a personal commitment to accomplish their own learning.

Your analysis of student characteristics (pages 30–31) can indicate needs that can best be served with this method. Students have opportunities to take increasing control of their own learning, often by using computer software. Applications include drill and practice with basic skills, tutoring activities, content-and-skills learning through games or contests, and simulations or experiments that replicate realistic situations. With well-designed software programs, a teacher can personalize and sequence learning tasks for individual students, based on assessments of prior knowledge and performance, while tracking each one's progress and maintaining records. Commercial programs that include these components may be called *individualized learning systems* (ILS). In addition, a student can log onto the Internet, search Web sites, and research any topic to satisfy assigned or selected learning objectives.

For students, developing a sense of responsibility and decision-making skills is among the important benefits derived from self-directed activities. Furthermore, we are moving to a level at which instructional technology can provide the capacity for some students to identify, design, and carry out plans for their own learning. By using personal computers with well-designed interactive software—that which includes still and animated images, text, and sound with branching and linking from one concept to another—the effect is that of a one-on-one personal tutor for each student. This can make learning more productive and effective.

A warning! While available resources for self-directed learning may reduce the need for classroom presentations, do not neglect group interaction experiences and other personal contacts that should follow up or supplement self-directed learning activities.

Self-directed learning programs, frequently called *self-study modules,* most often treat many of the planning components explained in this guidebook. The format may include:

- **Title** or reference number for the module's topic

- **Pretest** to determine a student's preparation for studying the topic, review or remedial work needed, and any present competencies within the topic's objectives that might be skipped

- **Goal or purpose** for studying the topic

- **Outline of key subject components** of the topic

- **Learning objectives** that specify outcomes in terms of required content, learning performance, and conditions

- **Learning activities and resources** (media, software, and print) as required for use or with alternatives for student selection

- **Self-administered tests** for a student to check his or her own learning level while proceeding through or completing the program, with any need to review, or as readiness to proceed to the teacher's evaluation

- **Post-test,** derived from objectives, to measure student learning, often with multiple forms that would permit retesting for mastery as necessary

- **Quest or application** in practical situations that allow the student to use information or further apply skills learned

Self-directed learning can be narrowly or broadly applied. Three methods may be used. (See Figure 6 on page 50.)

- **Method 1**—All students study the same objectives, following the same activities, using the same resources. Each student progresses at his or her own pace. At a preset time (for example, the end of the week), study must be completed, and a test is administered to all students.

- **Method 2**—While all students are to satisfy the same objectives for the topic, they may engage in various activities and select from a number of available resources, depending on individual needs, interests, and learning styles. As in Method 1, the evaluation takes place at the same time for all students.

- **Method 3**—Here each student selects or is assigned a set of objectives for the topic that is appropriate for him or her. Activities and resources for study are assigned or chosen by the student. Study takes place at the student's own pace, even with some individual control over the sequencing of objectives. Evaluation is conducted *when the student is ready to be tested on learning.*

The third method can provide a more flexible approach to instruction. It can allow the delivery of only as much content as the student needs, or for an advanced student, it may go beyond the essential information and extend learning further or in a new direction. Thus, a student can progress at an appropriate pace with material directly relevant to his or her level of learning. Then, through sequential, periodic testing, satisfactory learning can practically be guaranteed.

See Appendix B, Chapter 25 (pages 139–143) for an example of a school-level application of self-directed learning.

When starting to provide for extensive self-directed learning activities, a teacher may find it disconcerting to accept the fact that students are studying at different levels and even pursuing various topics. The classroom or laboratory atmosphere may seem chaotic at times. But there are benefits a teacher will recognize when self-directed activities become an integral part of an instructional program. Some of these benefits are:

- Freedom from routine teaching of basic facts and skills

- More time available to spend with individual students in diagnosing needs, setting paths for learning, giving help, and monitoring progress

- More opportunities to interact with students on higher intellectual levels concerning their problems, interests, and uses for the subject content

- Being available to direct and assist aides who help individual students

Sometimes a student may know more about a topic he or she is studying than does the teacher. Rather than viewing this as a troublesome situation, the teacher can use this experience as an opportunity to suggest that the student mentor other students.

While many advantages for using self-directed learning are recognized, there are some important limitations. First, locating and evaluating software programs and media materials, or developing them, require time and skill. The library media specialist should be helpful here (see page 60.) Second, if a single-path, lockstep method is used repeatedly, as in Method 1, learning may become monotonous and uninteresting for many students. Third, an emphasis on self-directed learning may not be appropriate initially for all students, based on their limited maturity, lack of readiness, or different preferred learning styles. Therefore, self-directed learning should be combined with the other instructional patterns in most programs so as to provide a number of ways for learning to take place.

GROUP ACTIVITIES: COOPERATIVE AND INTERACTIVE

In this pattern, teachers and students, or students themselves, work together in small groups to discuss,

FIGURE 6
Methods for Using Modules in Self-Directed Learning

Students	Method 1			Method 2			Method		
	A	B	C	A	B	C	A	B	C
*Modules	1	2	1	1a	1a	1b	6	1	8
	2		2	2b		2c	3	2	9
			1		2a	3a		3	
	3	3	3c	3a,c		5	4		
			3	4b		4b,c			5
	4	4			4c		8	6	
		5	4	5a	5a		Eval.	7	4
	5		5			5b		8	6
								Eval.	10
	Evaluation			Evaluation					Eval.

Letters represent different activities/resources for objectives (numbers).

engage in activities, and pursue a problem or project cooperatively. These are important features:

- Objectives in the affective and interpersonal domains, such as attitude formation, development of appreciation, cooperation, and sharing responsibilities, can be attained.

- In the cognitive domain, such high-level intellectual skills as making inferences, solving problems, and reaching decisions can receive attention.

Other values for students include:

- Practice in leadership functions.

- Experiences in listening and oral expression while organizing and presenting their ideas.

- More advanced students can strengthen their own learning by instructing and mentoring other students.

- Those who need encouragement can be recognized, and those making poor progress can be identified.

A number of different techniques may be used to encourage and provide for interaction within small groups. While planning, choices can be made from among these activities:

- Class discussion—face-to-face interactions in which facts, ideas, and opinions can be exchanged through questioning, providing information, and expressing individual positions.

- Panel discussion—two or more qualified persons (invited specialists or possibly students who have completed research on a topic) present information or their views on the topic to the class, followed by questions from the students.

- Buzz groups—small discussion groups consider the same or different topics or problems, then report back to the entire class with members reacting to the ideas presented.

- Case study—provide teams of students with detailed information about a real-life situation; they engage in study and analysis, reaching a conclusion with justification and defense of the team's position.

- Games—a competitive activity for a topic as teams apply a set of rules and procedures that require actions and decision making with immediate feedback, leading to a reachable goal and the proclaimed winner.

- Role playing and simulation—spontaneous dramatization involving the feelings and thoughts of real people as expressed by two or more persons relating to a situation or problem, followed by analysis and discussion with the class.

- Visualizations—encourage students in an activity to express their ideas in a visual format, such as pictures, illustrations, diagrams, objects, or computer-generated images.

- Computer use—two or three students interact together while studying a computer program, helping each other.

- Projects—individuals, teams, or groups of students work together cooperatively on an assigned or selected problem that requires defining a goal, deciding on objectives to accomplish, agreeing on actions to take within the group, assigning responsibilities, carrying out research, engaging in activities (often in the community), organizing information and findings, reaching conclusions, and preparing written and/or oral reports. (See the information on problem-based projects in Chapter 19 of Appendix A, pages 115–118, and the project application in Chapter 28 of Appendix B, pages 153–163. Also see Slavin's *Cooperative Learning: Theory, Research, and Practice*—listed in "References and Sources," Section H, page 167—which contains useful information for cooperative group project activities.)

While teachers would be familiar and experienced with most of these interactive activities, some of them, such as role playing and group projects, could be new and uncertain for students. Therefore, direct guidance and support from the teacher, at least in the early stages, may be necessary as students feel their way and develop confidence in their participation and responsibilities.

As with the other two patterns for teaching and learning, group activities have limitations and problems that must be recognized. Pre-session preparation by students is necessary so that all will participate and benefit from the activities. Encouraging interest, participation, and cooperation for all participants may require special guidance until confidence is developed. The teacher or group leader should also be prepared to control students who react emotionally or tend to monopolize the group's time.

SELECTING METHODS FOR INSTRUCTION AND LEARNING

The design plan being developed here can guide students, in a structured way, through learning specific, testable knowledge and skills. It can also allow students to direct some of their own learning with access to additional activities and resources. A major decision during planning is to decide which type of activity is most suitable for the subject content and each set of objectives for the topic. Selection should be based on the planning team's or teacher's answers to questions like these:

- Which instructional pattern, or combination of methods, is most suitable or preferred for each component of the topic's subject content and learning objectives?

- How can each category of required learning—low-level information or recall, psychomotor skills, higher-level intellectual learning, and affective/interpersonal objectives—be treated most effectively?

- How can such important practices and outcomes as inquiry-based learning, convergent and divergent thinking, collaborative problem solving, and interdependence be accomplished?

- To what extent can a student receive help on a topic or skip ahead if competence is already shown?

- How can a student's special interests and needs be best recognized and served?

(Also see the example of a new program's components and instructional methods in Chapter 16 of Appendix A on pages 105–108.)

When deciding on teaching and learning activities within each of the three teaching/learning patterns, consider these guidelines:

- Involve students in the planning.

- Decide responsibilities and activities for the teacher (presenter, interactive leader, selector of resources, consultant or guide to students, manager of aides, etc.).

- Guide each student's activities (plan, observe, study independently, interact, cooperate, etc.).

- Decide necessary resources for teacher and student uses (see Chapter 10).

- Decide on other personnel, including aides, parents, and those from the community, needed to assist or supplement the teacher in program activities (see Chapter 11).

- Assign necessary time periods for each activity. (For example, interdisciplinary theme presentations may require 30- to 45-minute periods coordinated with follow-up small-group activity sessions.)

For further details of logistical support services, see Chapter 11.

This approach to instruction and learning is much more complex than the traditional, teacher-centered, resource-limited, and time lockstep educational method. But these procedures are necessary for instruction and learning on the Stage 3 level of the McBeath model of educational change (Figure 1 on page 9).

Try not to allow conventional practices to control the mix of how teaching and learning *must* take place. Respond to this question: "Based on the learning objectives, what experiences do we want students to have so as to facilitate learning for each student?" This will require planning that should partially or wholly integrate traditional subject disciplines through interdisciplinary theme presentations with follow-up small-group reviews and applications, self-directed and cooperative learning, and problem-based projects, all operational within a flexible scheduled day.

Although each teacher has responsibilities for a "class" of students, consider how you can integrate activities among classes. For example, in theme study, a single teacher or a team can plan and make a series of presentations, using suitable resources, to a combined two to three classes of students. Then the students meet in small-group sessions under the leadership of teachers, aides, or even older students (high school or college level). This can become an efficient use of time, space, and teachers' efforts. See "References and Sources," Section H, page 167, for additional suggestions relating to instructional methods and learning activities.

A final question to answer is: "In view of this information on instructional methods and learning activities for accomplishing the objectives of a topic, what specific teacher instructional activities and what student learning activities should be implemented?"

As teachers consider this important question, see "The Mechanics of Planning" in Chapter 11 for how decisions on these two categories of activities can be structured and visually organized within the planning sequence. They start to lead to the formulation of lesson plans (sample on page 74). ◆

CHAPTER 10

Instructional Resources

▶ *What are the benefits of using conventional media and new technologies for instruction and learning?*

▶ *Into what groupings can media resources and new technologies be placed?*

▶ *What factors must be considered when selecting resources for instructional uses?*

▶ *How can you develop a technology plan for a school or a department?*

The advantages of using conventional types of media, cited and proven many years ago, are now extended with newer, computer-based technologies. Not only can they communicate information, explain, clarify, and illustrate concepts and principles, but they also can capture attention, hold interest, inspire, excite imagination, affect attitudes, and extend instruction beyond the immediate building through distance education and Internet access. Today we also recognize that many advanced technologies can serve other instructional needs, such as providing interaction, giving feedback, and reinforcing learning while contributing to increased productivity in teaching and learning.

This means much more than just adding technology to conventional education. These new resources can affect classroom dynamics, what is to be studied, where and how students can find information, and how they may engage in their studies. Sophisticated advantages of newer resources for student uses include:

• promoting student inquiry through involvement in interdisciplinary assignments

• simulating real-world environments so that students will be able to carry out authentic tasks and experimentations

• making accessible to students information that can be stored, analyzed, reorganized, and conveyed to other persons, and used in various ways

• allowing students to communicate with others and to participate from any location in collaborative projects

• supporting such higher-level intellectual skills as problem solving and critical thinking

Teachers' professional roles can also be supported and extended by technology. These include:

• acquiring more subject content, instructional knowledge, and teaching skills

• developing and tailoring instructional materials to specific learning needs

• having more time to assist individual students

• conducting ongoing assessments of student learning

- keeping detailed records of student progress

- communicating effectively with parents, other teachers, resource persons, and the public

CATEGORIES OF RESOURCES

Instructional resources can be grouped into a number of categories:

- Real things—guest speakers; life-size objects and devices

- Community resources—museums, libraries, natural settings, local agencies

- Simulated objects—models and simplified, enlarged replicas of structures or apparatus

- Display materials—chalkboards and flipcharts; bulletin boards; enlarged photographs; diagrams, charts, and graphs

- Paper products—printed paper and photocopies

- Audio recordings—audiocassettes, compact discs (CDs), software-generated sound

- Projected still pictures—overhead transparencies, slides, computer-generated images

- Projected images with motion—video recordings, videodiscs, compact discs (CD-ROMs)

- Computer software—programs for information, drill, and practice; simulations; games; applications; teachers' software for record keeping and administrative tasks; and desktop publishing, to include spreadsheets, drawing, painting, and graphing tools for individual use or for group-interaction activities

- Multimedia (combinations of media)—audio recording with slides; audio recording with printed materials; computer control of text, audio, graphics, slides, and video, in any integrated combination for both individual study and group projection uses

- Electronic databases—bodies of information that allow students to access, organize, and manipulate data

- Hypermedia—information structured as nodes or frames, with links that allow for rapid movement through the information in a flexible order

- Electronic distance learning—closed circuit, cable, or satellite-system television; amplified and video telephone; e-mail; and networks for obtaining and sharing information and for the distribution of traditional courses that are not available locally, or as enrichment opportunities for advanced students, from a single site to multiple remote local, regional, or global locations; in addition, distance learning can enable teachers to conveniently participate in professional development activities (see the publication *Improving Education through Distributed Learning*, listed in "References and Sources," Section I, page 168).

Resources for electronic learning are emerging as major forces in education. Many of the conventional media forms, such as slides and overhead transparencies, are increasingly being computer-generated rather than prepared by hand or photographically. This allows for display to take place directly from computer memory via an electronic display unit. Computer-based images and software programs can be used for instructional and learning activities in all three patterns: presentation, self-directed learning, and interactive group activities. For practical experience, students in vocational training can use the same software found in the workplace. They may create spreadsheets to analyze data for science and math projects, and use a PowerPoint-type program to design slides for a report or presentation. (See Dockterman, "Reference and Sources," Section I, page 168, for suggestions for computer uses in each teaching/learning pattern.)

We recognize the concept of networking for sharing information and the offerings of the Internet for many instructional purposes. Your school has (or will have) a local-area network (LAN) that connects computers within the building. The network can be expanded throughout the school district and into the community, becoming a wide-area network (WAN). Then the whole world opens to unlimited communication and information searches via the Internet, which allows teachers and students to do much of the following:

- Exchange e-mail and interact with other teachers, students, and resource people relating to projects and interests.

- Search for and retrieve library resources and electronic databases from numerous locations when gathering information or conducting research.

- Acquire and share up-to-date information with and from other specialized sources via the World Wide Web (WWW) that may contain text, graphics, sound, and even video with animation.

- Create an online school Web page about the new program and projects underway, inviting interaction and input.

Technology choices can best be made as instructional methods and learning activities are selected. Keep in mind that restructuring the school day away from conventional, lockstep periods to more flexible use of time for presentations, self-directed learning, and small-group activities can be facilitated with increased use of new technologies. This means that the necessary resources and student training in their use should be conveniently available whenever they are needed.

SELECTING RESOURCES FOR INSTRUCTION

Choose one or more resources when you believe they can make positive contributions to learning. Do not neglect older, less expensive media forms, such as textbooks with worksheets or audiocassette recordings, which could be effective ways to engage students' minds. When selecting resources for specific teaching and learning activities, consider special features, called *attributes*, of the various resources:

- Situation for use—class presentation, group interaction, or for self-paced learning

- Treatment required of subject—real or symbolic/verbal

- Pictorial representation—photographic or graphic

- Factor of size—non-projected or projected

- Factor of color—black and white or color

- Factor of movement—still or motion, live action, or animation

- Factor of language—oral sound, printed words, or multilingual

- Sound/picture relationship—silent picture or image with sound

- Set or variable order of images—linear sequence or flexible order by choice of teacher or student, or controlled by computer software program

- Interactive qualities—participation, group interchange, Web interactions

- Location of necessary resources for use—in the classroom, laboratory, or elsewhere in the building; in the community; or at a distance or remote site

- Availability of training for teachers and students

When judging educational materials and programs for use, remember that their subject treatment and production quality may be compared by students with what they see on commercial television and encounter in computer games. The creativity, professional production values, and fast action that they experience with those media can influence responses to educational materials.

Based on the above attributes, ask yourself this important question: "According to the nature of subject content for the topic and the requirements of learning objectives, which resource(s) would best serve the chosen teaching/learning methods?"

Then, to reach a final media decision, respond to these questions:

- Does the needed material already exist in suitable form and quality?

- What quantity of individual items would be needed?

- How much would purchase or preparation cost?

- What would be the reproduction or duplication costs, if any? (Note copyright protection.)

- How much time would be required to locate or prepare the material?

- What would be the production requirements for equipment, facilities, and technical skills?

- Does the teacher have a preference for use?

- Would one medium be more suitable than others because of ease of use or handling by students?

- Would there be any problems regarding equipment, facilities, storage, supervision, and scheduling for use?

STUDENT-PREPARED MATERIALS

As we move students toward higher levels of activities for learning, they will engage in preparing both a variety and a quantity of their own materials. These can be brief outlines and writings; a diary, log, or journal of activities, including decisions made with supporting evidence; more lengthy reports; visual materials such as diagrams, artwork, photographs, and displays; possibly slide, video, or even computer-based presentations; and copies of material sent and received via e-mail or the Internet. Preparing such materials has many advantages for students and can provide them with beneficial learning experiences.

Students can be guided to do very creative things with computers, including designing illustrations, scanning print and images into memory, and com-

bining text with graphics. Also by using authoring software, students can plan and design sophisticated interactive programs that may include photographs, video, and sound, and pages for publication or display. Sometimes it may be best for a teacher to step aside and let a student's curiosity and enthusiasm take over!

When planning and selecting activities to serve learning objectives, ask yourself the following question: "With which resources can students have beneficial hands-on experiences?"

As students increasingly use Web sites, they should be guided to:

- develop Web navigation skills for ease of use

- identify age-appropriate sites for better understanding of content

- recognize the reliability of a site to provide accurate information

- credit the source providing the information used in homework or a report

The materials students prepare or collect can become the contents of a collection or a *portfolio* for each student. It can be designed to contain a variety of items that reveal how a student's knowledge and abilities change, grow, and mature toward predetermined goals and planned objectives. The contents may be connected to activities relating to presentations, self-directed learning, and interactive group work. For the student, a sense of ownership and accomplishment can result. The portfolio also is an excellent resource to share with parents. Criteria for purposes, content, and evaluation standards should be clear to both teachers and students. (See portfolio evaluation criteria in Chapter 12.)

A SCHOOL TECHNOLOGY PLAN

As an increasing variety of more sophisticated technological resources becomes essential in educational programs, a school must broaden its traditional library services to provide for many new instructional needs, including online cataloguing, interactive multimedia resources, and even resource sharing. The concept today of a school's technology-support program is much broader than the old-style belief that the school library is a cafeteria in which teachers and students help themselves to whatever resources are available. The McBeath Stage 3 model, with its principles, practices, and outcomes (page 9), should be recognized in the technology support area, just as it is in the curriculum design and instructional implementation areas.

Technology support committee

Initially, the project planning team, along with the school library media specialist, can serve as the steering group for examining the present print and media resources and services, recommending any necessary changes and extensions. The project instructional designer and one or more technical specialists also should be on the committee. In time, other interested teachers, parents, and community representatives may be added to the group or replace initially active persons.

As in the process for planning for transforming an educational program, which starts with a vision statement and mission goals (pages 35–36), decide what purposes and services should be provided by the school's technology program. This may be termed a *strategic plan for technology*. It provides guidelines for the services, personnel, and activities to support the new program.

Services and resources

As a start, consider these necessary activities with potential budgetary requirements:

- The balance between providing a computer learning lab associated with the media center and installations in classrooms

- New hardware, including personal computers, scanners, printers, and facsimile machines, with some upgrades expected every three years and possible replacement of various items after five years

- New software installed for use in instruction with periodic reevaluations and upgrades

- Local- and wide-area networks (LANs and WANs) with satellite facilities and cabling throughout the school, with access beyond the school into the community

- Technical support for installations, maintenance, and repair

- In-service training (formal and casual) of teachers, aides, and students for acquiring information and skills; this training may require release time, voluntary consultants, or employment of specialists

With the necessary and increasing attention being given to computer-based resources, do not neglect the need for conventional print and visual formats, which continue to have useful roles in instruction.

Personnel

The extent of the program and its services will require qualified personnel in a number of areas. Consider which services could be handled by the library media specialist, often in close coordination with the instructional designer, and which will necessitate other individuals, possibly competent persons from the community.

Among the services that may be required are the following:

- Coordination, management, and handling of ongoing changes in the school's communication installations; organization of available space; acquisition of hardware and software; and training of teachers, staff, and students to use the resources

- Locating reference and information resources that can serve the objectives of curriculum topics and themes, and assisting with establishing evaluation criteria as resources are considered; acquiring the necessary materials in sufficient quantities, cataloging them, and making them available for use

- Continual maintenance of all electronic equipment

- Preparation of materials for use in teacher presentations, displays, group sessions, or by individual students in self-directed learning activities

- Assistance and supervision of students as they prepare materials for group or individual projects; while teachers and other students can help with such production activities, more experienced persons with special knowledge and abilities may be needed

- Services of students to provide logistical support to teachers for using equipment and even some technical maintenance by competent upper-grade students

Some important activities

- Provide cataloguing and checkout for materials and equipment to students and teachers.

- In addition to regular school hours of operation, consider providing services before and after school.

- Provide information access through a wide range of databases and other software reference resources.

- Coordinate support of selected distance learning programs for teachers and some students that allow all participants to see and hear each other.

- Ensure availability of laptop computers for student checkout and home use.

- Help students to become critical information consumers.

- Apply practices of acceptable uses for software that recognize intellectual freedom, copyright and fair use guidelines, and ethical concerns.

- Provide adequate physical storage, inventory, and security of equipment and resources within school facilities.

Fiscal requirements

Based on planned or anticipated new program needs, as described above, the support committee should identify costs for facilities adaptation, new equipment, materials, and support services. Some items will be a one-time cost, while others will require a yearly budget as the program becomes operational. Funds can be requested from the school district, public and private grant sources, or through special allocations (private contributions or possibly a bond issue). For more information on grant sources, see "References and Sources," Section N, page 169.

FINAL OBSERVATIONS

Recognize that new technological resources can make positive contributions as they are integrated into an instructional program utilizing the systematic planning process described here. Within this process, students must be guided to become technologically literate—that means to develop dexterity within present and emerging technologies, and to become comfortable with using specific resources wisely, creatively, and effectively.

Also be prepared to serve additional teachers and students. As sophisticated and innovative new technologies continue to be developed at an ever increasing rate, the process of funding, selection, evaluation, installation, training, and use will be an ongoing concern.

For helpful suggestions and further details on many concepts relating to developing a school's technology program, see these four references: Brody, Craver, Donham, and the Ohio Schools Technology Implementation Task Force ("References and Sources," Section I, pages 167–168).   ◆

CHAPTER 11

Instructional Logistics and Program Support

▶ *To support an instructional program, what seven matters need consideration?*

▶ *How can a budget be developed within two categories?*

▶ *What facilities, materials, and equipment will be necessary for use in the new program?*

▶ *What personnel, with what competencies, should become involved in the program?*

▶ *How can the new program be scheduled and coordinated with other school activities?*

▶ *What procedures can be used to handle the mechanics of the planning process?*

Depending on the level and complexity of your project, limited or extensive support (beyond what is conventionally available to a teacher) may be needed. In this chapter, we consider important services that should be examined. As you read, ask yourself what bearing each service may have on your project, and to what depth it should be treated.

In the early stage of planning, recognition was given to certain constraints within which a program may have to be developed (see pages 36–37). Relating to these constraints, necessary support should be carefully specified as planning proceeds and especially as teaching/learning activities and resources are selected. Consider these matters for satisfactory instructional support :

- Budget
- Facilities
- Materials
- Equipment
- Personnel services
- Time allocations and schedules
- Coordination with other school programs and activities

BUDGET

Most often, a new program requires special funding with which to get started. Initially, this is for planning time, program development, and other preparatory services. While the school or district might absorb the cost for the time that you and other individuals devote to planning functions, or for the services of one or more outside consultants, many of the following will require financial support during planning development:

- Professional planning time

- Clerical support time

- Costs of consultative services

- Additions to or renovation of necessary facilities

- Purchase of equipment, its installation and necessary wiring, and operational support

- Purchase or preparation of instructional materials, including professional research and planning time, in-school technical and production services or outside vendor services, raw materials, duplication, packaging for multiple copies, and online cataloguing

- Development of testing instruments for evaluation of student learning for formative evaluation (Chapter 12) and eventually for evaluation of program results (summative evaluation; see Chapter 13)

- Costs for tryouts, including personnel time and consumable materials

- Time to train teachers and staff for implementation phase

- Administration time for coordination and supervision

- Administrative costs (travel, telephone, e-mail and Internet, overhead, etc.)

In addition to district-supplied money, special grants may be necessary to plan, develop, and start up a new program. Such funds may need to be requested shortly after the idea for the new program is first considered. Also, instead of committing to immediate large expenditures for equipment, consider leasing or making payments over the life of expensive items. The instructional design plan presented in this guidebook can become a sound framework for a funding proposal.

Identify support-fund sources for submitting proposals. (See potential sources listed in Section N of "References and Sources," page 169.) Besides state, federal, foundation, and corporate funding, local private-sector resources, including money, equipment, and personnel or technical services, may be offered or can be requested. A specific plan might be developed to interest community businesses, organizations, and even special individuals to provide support for school improvement activities. (Refer to suggestions for preparing a Request for Proposal [RFP] to obtain technology resources, as described in Murphy and Schiller, pages 157–172, listed in "References and Sources," Section B, page 165.)

After tryout, with successful student accomplishments of learning objectives as the instructional program is implemented, hopefully it will be supported as an ongoing part of regular budgetary allocations. As compared with conventional school programs, some portions of operational costs for continued implementation may require increased funding for aides to assist teachers and greater amounts of hardware and software instructional resources. Administrators from school systems with nationally recognized technology programs agree that a district should devote about 3 percent of its annual operating budget to technology (see "Many Schools Rush to Get Wired without a Plan," *USA Today*, October 8, 1996, page 6D). Therefore, consider how to acquire additional long-term necessary funding for implementation to sustain and even extend your school reform efforts.

For accountability purposes, including measures to determine cost efficiency during program operation, record costs for these financial categories:

- Faculty and staff salaries

- Part-time pay for aides and other support persons

- Support for further necessary training

- Replacement of consumable and damaged materials

- Servicing and maintenance of equipment

- Depreciation of equipment

- Overhead costs for facilities and services

- For continuous improvement, revising and updating the program as required (personnel time, equipment, materials)

As a school program shifts toward recognition of the principles, practices, and outcomes in Stage 3 of the McBeath model of educational change (Figure 1 on page 9), the school district office itself may have to make adjustments in its operational and financial functions to make more efficient use of funds and resources. Such savings may be needed to support new school programs on an ongoing basis.

▶ *Which of the cost items noted for development and implementation do you consider necessary, and how would you proceed to satisfy them?*

FACILITIES

There is evidence of a direct connection between the setting in which students learn and the quality of their education. Such matters as these may need consideration when facilities are examined:

- The condition of the school building as an inviting facility with necessary security for safety of students and teachers

- The use of natural light where feasible, rather than artificial light

- Depending on geographic location, air conditioning as a more comfortable environment (68°–74° F)

- Flexible classroom arrangements to enable teachers to team up for larger class-presentation sessions, and allow for small-group sessions

- Arrangements in classrooms or in separate labs for individual student study and use of computers during self-directed learning activities

- Desks that are adjustable to accommodate growing students, and to hold books, a notebook, and even a laptop computer

- Electrical outlets available everywhere

Facilities to carry out an instructional program may require any of the following:

- Regular homeroom environment for 25 to 30 students

- Room for large-group presentations—up to 100 students—with a sound system, media projection equipment, and wiring for telephone, computer connection, and input from a satellite television receiver

- A necessary number of self-directed study stations (carrels or open tables) of a suitable size to hold equipment and study materials for student use; provision for sufficient electrical power, telephone connections (modems), necessary wiring, and circuits for computer network applications; and, depending on the number of computer installations, upgraded heating, ventilation, and air conditioning systems as needed

- Small-group meeting rooms (or areas with informal arrangements of furniture that may be adaptable in regular classrooms) for teacher-student and student-student work and interactions; these rooms or areas should be equipped with display surfaces (chalkboards, bulletin boards, flipcharts) and provisions for media projection

- The school library or a media resource center where materials and equipment are gathered, organized, and made available to teachers and students

- Staff meeting room and workroom

When deciding on facilities with equipment for a learning center (or an area in a classroom) to serve self-directed learning uses, consider these questions:

- How many students are to be served at one time?

- How much time will a student probably spend in the center?

- For how many hours per day will the center be available for use?

Based on the answers to these questions, and considering the funds available, decide on the number of required stations and equipment.

As the need for specific facilities is recognized, consider which available rooms can be used without modification and which ones require minor or major adaptations. Ideas for renovating present facilities can be obtained by contacting and visiting other schools or training facilities in nearby companies, which may have installed similar facilities. It can be useful to consult with qualified experts who know about space needs for various activities, electrical requirements and wiring, and other technical matters.

▶ *In terms of the potential needs of the project, what uses can be made of each available room or area, and what modifications or extensive renovations may be necessary?*

MATERIALS

Once the resources needed to support activities have been decided, it will be necessary to locate and acquire specific commercial items or to prepare materials. If materials are to be prepared, then a planning and production sequence for media, including video and computer-based multimedia items, should be followed. Setting objectives, outlining content, storyboarding, and scripting (with teacher approval at each step), followed by preparing graphics (taking pictures or videotaping) and sound recording, usually are necessary. When the original material has been completed, edited, and accepted, a sufficient number of duplicate copies for teacher and student uses will need to be made. Other required materials, including printed items such as directions and information sheets, study guides, worksheets, and workbooks, will need to be written and prepared, or enough copies obtained for the number of students to be served.

(For assistance with any phases of media planning and production, refer to Kemp and Smellie, listed in "References and Sources," Section I, page 168.)

▶ *What decisions and actions should be taken or made concerning materials needed in the program?*

EQUIPMENT

Is proper, sufficient equipment already available, or must it be obtained? (The three questions listed under "Facilities" on page 65 can help with this answer in support of self-directed learning activities.)

Here again, expert help may be advisable. Find out what kinds of equipment have proven to be easy to use and durable. Be aware that computers are dropping in price and inexpensive models are becoming available with sufficient memory, speed, and necessary features so that increased numbers of them can be made available to students. Do not leave the final decision on equipment to consultants. Those teachers and aides to be involved in a new program should themselves carefully examine and work with whatever equipment is recommended. Have some students also use the equipment before you make a final decision. Each teacher participating in the new programs should have direct access to a personal computer. More important, it should be on his or her desk for use at any time as an administrative tool or an instructional aid.

Please note: Schools that plan to acquire used computers contributed by business concerns or individuals may find the donations of limited value. An organization composed of business leaders and educators advises accepting used computers only if it would cost less than $500 to upgrade each machine to run current software. Also, schools can trim the cost of tapping into the World Wide Web by teaming up with local businesses and nonprofit organizations to become part of their networks. Finally, at the time new equipment is purchased or obtained through a grant, plan how teachers and aides, or even students, will be trained to use it.

▶ *What equipment and support are needed for the program? How might items be obtained?*

PERSONNEL CAPABILITIES

For more extensive new programs (entire courses, overall department restructuring, or total school transformation), the site-based, comprehensive, and systematic planning process being developed here needs a high level of collaboration from and coordination among many individuals and groups. The commitment of their time, energy, and resources is required for successful school transformation. In addition, there may be specialists and other support persons who should be called upon for their services.

Teachers

Those teachers who initially participate in program development should exhibit certain traits and behaviors. It is important that they have a perspective on educational change that fits within the principles, practices, and outcomes in Stage 3 of the McBeath model (Figure 1 on page 9). At the beginning of the process, teachers may not recognize or accept all factors listed in the McBeath model, but they should be open to changes and broadening viewpoints. Also review the suggestions on pages 26–27 about forming the planning team and personal behaviors for planning. Here are some other qualities that project participants should have or be able to develop:

- a dissatisfaction with the present educational situation, leading to a sincere interest in making major changes

- the ability to work with students at each student's level of experience

- a concern with guiding students toward success in learning (doing things *with*, not *to*, students)

- a motivation level that is not "just talk," but indicates their readiness to take action

- a desire to be creative by exploring new ideas and fresh instructional techniques

- a willingness to cooperate as a team member

- an interest in acquiring an understanding of, and developing competencies in, the systematic planning process described here (or an equally useful approach)

- subject-matter knowledge and above-average teaching competencies

- a high level of awareness of or skills with new technological resources

- a willingness to explore and continue learning related to many of the qualities listed here

- a commitment to participate until satisfactory results are attained

In addition to direct teaching responsibilities, each member of the team will play an active part in:

- motivating students to acquire knowledge and improve their learning skills

- monitoring student progress

- diagnosing learning difficulties and providing each student with corrective measures

- recognizing good performance and offering encouragement

- supervising the work of assistants or aides

- communicating with parents about student progress or difficulties

- mentoring other teachers who become active in the new program

Teachers also should become proficient in networking, either directly or through the Internet, with other teachers and useful professional contacts. These connections can reveal sources for topic content and new instructional ideas. Because many of the skills teachers will need may be new, the plans for professional development, in-service workshops, visits to see other innovative programs, opportunities to examine and select both hardware and software, and to practice media uses must be considered. In recognition of these "additional time" matters, teachers should receive support through release time and/or grant funds when feasible.

▶ *How do you and other teachers in the project respond to the above competencies and experiences indicated for teachers? If you find some deficiencies exhibited by members of the planning team, how might they be overcome?*

Program administrator/coordinator or facilitator

The school principal or coordinator within the planning team also should understand and accept the Stage 3 concepts in the McBeath model (Figure 1 on page 9) appropriate for the Information Age, while providing administrative leadership and program support. He or she should be forward looking and have the ability to inspire co-workers. On more practical levels, this person would be responsible for arranging schedules, making personnel assignments, handling equipment and budget allocations, and obtaining necessary facilities as the program moves from planning into development and then implementation.

The coordinator should have a number of abilities and areas of experience that contribute to both leadership and management responsibilities:

- Vision of future needs, commitment to facilitator role, ability to work cooperatively with others

- Knowledge of the change process and how to help others prepare for and handle change

- Being proactive by taking the initiative and anticipating needs and problems

- Group process skills—planning and running meetings, conducting discussions, helping the planning group make decisions

- Interpersonal skills—listening, questioning, providing feedback, offering encouragement, supporting suggestions, managing conflicts

- Presentation skills—delivering information, using media resources, replying to questions

- Planning process—handling stages of the planning process as outlined here or as modified early in planning, coordinating with an instructional designer (as explained in the next section), and managing time effectively

- Data handling—gathering, analyzing, summarizing, reporting, and sharing plans, progress, and results

- Working with consultants, higher-level administrators, parents, community representatives, and others, keeping in mind the question, "What do we want from them?"

  —verbal or actual support?

  —financial support?

  —advice and/or direct participation?

  —allocation of resources?

  —other contributions?

- Expressing an attitude that is nonthreatening, while encouraging trust, cooperation, experimentation, and risk taking

- Preparing teachers and other staff to face criticism, and offering help in finding ways to cope with disagreements

- Deciding when and how to involve additional teachers and students in transformational activities

- Financial responsibilities—preparing proposals for funds; obtaining funds; handling budget, purchases, and expenses; being alert to financial flow, budget balances, and expense deadlines

- Recognizing the need to manage the "politics" associated with introducing a new program into an organization; this would include:

  —encouraging and supporting teachers and students to engage in nonconventional activities

  —obtaining permission or clearance for materials, equipment, and facilities

  —being alert to human conflicts; supporting necessary staff requests or actions

  —keeping all necessary persons informed as the project proceeds

▶ *Who should fill this essential role in your project?*

Instructional designer

The instructional planning method being presented in this guidebook goes beyond conventional curriculum planning. Therefore, someone who understands and is experienced in applying a systematic planning process should have a leadership role. This person must have a background in instructional systems design (ISD) and be familiar with published works such as those listed in "References and Sources," Section E (page 166). Furthermore, knowledge of educational philosophy, learning psychology, the communications process, instructional and evaluation methodologies, and experience with both conventional and new instructional technologies is essential. (Follow the description and activities of the instructional designer in the program being transformed in Appendix A, starting on page 95.)

With the appropriate beliefs, knowledge, and experience, the role of the instructional designer may be filled by a school administrator or a qualified teacher—someone who may also fit within the Program Administrator/Coordinator or Facilitator personnel category. This role requires an awareness of shifts in thinking relative to education for this Information Age, as envisioned in the McBeath model (Figure 1 on page 9). At least in the early planning phase, it may be preferred to have an instructional design specialist in the project. Many graduate programs in instructional technology, usually within a university school of education, train educators in this specialty. Check with your local university's education school or a national organization that serves such specialists (such as the Association for Educational Communications and Technology, AECT, *www.aect.org*).

▶ *Who can best fill this important role for your planning group?*

Consultants and specialists

When necessary, persons with knowledge and competencies in special subject areas, computer skills, emerging electronic technologies, evaluation of student learning, and measuring program results, should be called upon for advice, guidance, and service as needs are recognized.

▶ *What consultants are, or might become, necessary as the program develops?*

Other educational gatekeepers

Behind the actions of the planning team to initiate and carry through the planning, must be the commitment of higher-level administrators—the school principal (if not directly involved already), district superintendent, other administrative staff members, and the elected school board. Support from these leaders can be evidenced by:

- expressing an interest by meeting with planning personnel and then visiting the operative program during tryout and implementation

- responding to progress reports with commendation, questions, or recommendations

- responding to requests for additional personnel services and resource support

- telling others (legislators, business, and community leaders) about the new program

- including comments about the program in media interviews, public presentations, and when meeting other district educators

(Further recommendations for program management are included in Chapter 14.)

▶ *If you are an administrator, how do you respond to the attitudes, abilities, and procedures presented in this chapter? How might you acquire some of the skills and interpersonal relations if inadequacies are identified?*

Support personnel

Library and media professionals; materials preparation and equipment technicians; aides to assist teachers as tutors, proctors, or facilitators; and secretarial/clerical personnel all may have important functions in the new program. (See the descriptions under "Personnel" on page 60). An example of useful support is a school librarian who has access via the computer to the Educational Resources Information Centers (ERIC) around the country. ERIC's 16 centers collect and disseminate information on topics and practices relating to the school change process and curriculum areas.

Even older public school and college students may be scheduled to work with younger ones in phases of the new program. And do not forget the important role of school custodians and maintenance personnel in supporting a new program!

▶ *What support persons might you call on for services in the program?*

Parents

There is extensive evidence to show that when parents are actively involved in their child's education, the student is more successful in school. This can mean recognition, encouragement, and support at home, and also active parental participation at the school.

Parents should have important roles in various aspects of any school program. One responsibility of educators is to encourage parents to willingly participate. As indicated earlier, volunteers or selected parents should be involved in school advisory committees, on the planning team from the very beginning, and as volunteers. Because of their knowledge and experience, certain parents can serve as useful resources for student project activities. And hopefully, many parents can be encouraged to assist in instructional support functions.

Motivating parents to participate in these activities is a continuing concern for educators. Because of their many family- and work-related responsibilities, heavy schedules, and personal interests, it can be difficult for mothers and fathers to become actively involved in the school. For this reason, it may be a good idea to ask teachers to be available on some early mornings or evenings to meet with working parents for whom normal daytime appointments are not possible.

In addition, communicating with parents through student take-home announcements is often ineffective. Consider direct mail, such as personal letters and school newsletters (possibly prepared in part by students), e-mail messages, and follow-up phone calls. Plan school events that involve parents actively with their children. Also consider school programs that provide helpful services for parents, such as offering a series of workshops on good parenting practices and helping students with homework. Schedule basic computer-use classes for parents, possibly taught by qualified students. Through the cooperation of community agencies, provide information on available family services. Some schools are starting to provide e-mail connections and Web pages that allow parents to find out about school happenings, check their child's schoolwork, and even to contact individual teachers. All of these efforts can make parents more aware of school functions and encourage them to become more active in the school.

Additional useful suggestions on the following topics, relating to parents, are offered by Warner (see "References and Sources," Section L, page 169).

- Identifying family types

- Involvement strategies for different types of families

- Involvement areas for family and community

- Barriers to involvement

- Connecting parents with at-home support

- Connecting students and parents with in-school involvement

- Involvement to get bond issues passed

Older adults, such as retired persons who may be grandparents or have no children in school, can be encouraged to serve as aides or tutors. Sharing their experiences, knowledge, and skills with students often helps to make some curriculum topics more interesting and meaningful. A school can benefit immensely from the participation of such persons. There also can be many advantages to the individuals who volunteer, such as physical and mental activity, satisfaction in working with the teachers and students, and meeting other persons having similar interests. Contact local senior centers, invite participation through newspaper articles, and send out word-of-mouth requests.

▶ *In what specific ways might you actively encourage and motivate parents and other adults to become more involved in local school affairs?*

Community representatives

Community representatives, including business leaders and union representatives, should have a shared commitment for the school's success. They can be called on to provide policy, administrative, subject-matter, vocational, and technical support and to assist with student mentoring and tutoring. Encourage local companies to allow flexible scheduling for employees, so parents can visit the school during the workday. Career training for students might be provided through co-op programs, apprenticeships, internships, and other student hands-on experiences in the community. The following individuals and organizations can be encouraged to have closer links with the school:

- political leaders on local and state levels

- religious leaders

- social, health, and human-service organizations

- law enforcement agencies

- business leaders and company employees

- local higher-education faculty, including teacher education staff and students

- print and broadcast media representatives

- neighborhood residents

Additional information about community involvement with the school is provided in Chapter 6, pages 31–33. For suggestions on developing mutually beneficial alliances through school/business partnerships, refer to publications by Otterbourg and Warner in "References and Sources," Section L, page 169.

▶ *What persons in your community might be approached to participate . . . and for what purposes?*

Students

And, finally, the students—possibly we should have listed them first! The approach to education being presented here requires cooperation and a willingness on the part of students to participate. Handling their responsibilities, taking the initiative when feasible, making choices and decisions, and becoming confident, self-directed learners are important experiences for students. Many of them may not be mature enough or at a readiness level to fulfill their new roles immediately. Support and encouragement, with careful guidance, will be essential as students learn to shift their thinking and behaviors from Stages 1 and 2 to Stage 3 of the McBeath model of educational change (Figure 1 on page 9)—from dependence toward interdependence.

In the new self-directed component of the program (see Chapter 9, pages 48–50), students should be helped to assume responsibility for completing their assignments within a given time period. In scheduling student time, be alert to the tendency that some will procrastinate on their responsibilities. Therefore, set required times with the students for progress reports and deadlines to complete work, make reports, and take tests. Also recognize the additional assistance and time required by students with learning disabilities.

▶ *What characteristics of students in the program (as introduced on pages 30–31) need consideration as their roles and activities are planned?*

TIME ALLOCATIONS AND SCHEDULES

When a new project is approved, time is required for professional planning, for staff and clerical assistance in locating and preparing materials, and for support services to adapt facilities and install equipment. After the planning is completed, schedules are set for trying out the program. During the same period, time should be scheduled for staff orientation and training, as necessary. Finally, work schedules must be drawn up for teachers, aides, and students in order to put the instructional program into operation.

Answers to the following four questions become important:

- Should adjustment be made in the length of the regular school day, and even the academic year? (probably flexible with some longer daily periods)

- How should daily time be allocated among the presentation, group interaction, and self-directed learning phases of the new program? (This would require discontinuing the usual 45- to 50-minute repetitive periods during the day.)

- Should a team of teachers remain with a group of students for two to three years, so that lengthy sequences of instruction for the same students can take place?

- When can time be scheduled for teacher planning and project progress review sessions as the new program is implemented?

To see how a new program can be scheduled, refer to the weekly example on page 108 in Appendix A, and to the daily schedule on page 136 in Appendix B.

▶ *Which of the above questions, and what other ones, may need consideration by your planning team as program and activity schedules are developed?*

COORDINATION WITH OTHER SCHOOL PROGRAMS AND ACTIVITIES

If a new program will operate alongside conventional programs in a school, it may be treated as if it occupies a special world of its own. It may be given preference over regular classes in using facilities, and its participants may seem to have special privileges that other teachers and students know little about or may even resent. To avoid this situation, coordination and communication with others in the building can contribute to understanding and thus maintain good feelings.

Now consider the needs within your new program for all the logistical matters and support services presented here within each topic. With the consideration of these logistical and support matters, you are prepared to formulate details to complete lesson plans. (See the partial sample in Figure 7 on page 74. Note particularly the headings that are used.)

THE MECHANICS OF PLANNING

Here is a procedure that members of a planning team may find helpful. As you proceed, you will recognize that planning instruction is a complex process consisting of many interrelated, progressive sequences. This requires keeping in mind the elements raised by the 16 questions on pages 16–17 and continuous evaluation of the relationship of each part of the plan to the whole, because each element can affect the development of other ones. Insights gained in later planning stages often lead to revisions of earlier ones. Therefore, as you proceed, you will find that changes, deletions, reordering of items, and additions may be necessary. Maintaining an open mind and being flexible are essential throughout the planning process.

When one wants to express and hold on to intellectual thoughts, such ideas, plans, and procedures are usually put on paper (often through the vehicle of computer word processing or spreadsheets). However, a sheet of paper or a computer frame is a very limiting medium for use in instructional planning. Such lists or outlines are static, and making changes or shifting details around become difficult.

You can write on a chalkboard and add entries or erase unnecessary ones as you proceed, but this is inconvenient and cumbersome. Some teachers are comfortable with writing on large sheets of butcher paper displayed on an easel. This is another limiting surface, as it lacks flexibility. Both procedures require copying onto paper for ease of handling and further deskwork.

A preferred method is to do your initial planning on index cards (4x6 size is recommended) and display them on a tackboard or other display surface, or to use adhesive-backed Post-it® notes and stick them to a wall. On a separate card or note, boldly print the title of each planning component introduced in Figure 2 on page 18. Then write a single item on a card and place it under the appropriate heading as you proceed. You might even use different color cards or note sheets to differentiate the various planning elements. The cards are convenient to handle and exhibit for sharing, reviewing, and storing.

Numbering system used on planning cards

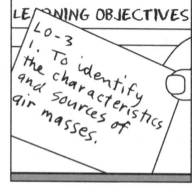

This procedure can be most helpful when designing the details of a topic as specified in the boxes for the Development phase of planning (as shown in Figure 2 on page 18). Start with the curriculum topic; then outline the subject content on cards under its heading. Follow with the learning objectives, each expressing the learning requirements of subject-content elements and placed horizontally alongside the related content cards. A series of objectives and content for the topic would be displayed vertically. Then continue horizontally to specify how each objective determines activities (teacher and student), resources, support services, and evaluation (post-test and pretest). Use numbering or some other identification method to identify and place each card in the plan sequence. Moving and rearranging cards, adding new items, and deleting entries can easily be done. This provides the flexibility you need in planning. And with this display, you can visually share the details with other members of the planning team as you proceed.

You may think this explanation for using cards and other matters in handling the mechanics of planning is unnecessary. But comprehensive instructional planning is a complex, creative process that requires keeping many separate elements in mind, seeing their relationships, and reevaluating the sequence and flow among the various elements. Writing those elements on cards and displaying them, as may be done in a flowcharting or storyboarding procedure, are practical ways to express your thoughts and organize necessary information in a usable, flexible form. Colleagues can easily see the plan for a topic as it develops, and changes leading to refinements are easy to make. (See the example below.)

As segments of planning are completed and accepted, the information on cards or note slips can be transferred to paper, as a working copy, using a spreadsheet computer software program. (For further details on handling these mechanics of planning, see Chapter 13 of *The Instructional Design Process* by Kemp, listed in "References and Sources," Section E, page 166.) ◆

Subject Content	Learning Objectives	Instructor Activities	Student Activities	Support Services	Evaluation	Pretest
SC–1	LO–1	IA–1	SA–1	SS–1	E–1	P–1
SC–2	LO–2		SA–2	SS–2	E–2	
SC–3	LO–3		SA–3	SS–3	E–3	P–3
SC–4a	LO–4	IA–4	SA–4		E–4	P–4
SC–4b						
SC–5	LO–5	IA–5	SA–5		E–5	

Example of a numbering system on planning cards

FIGURE 7

A Sample Lesson Plan *(partial subject treatment)*

Industrial Revolution—*Interdisciplinary theme* (see page 46)

Content Headings Presentation	Teacher Activity	Student Activity	Resources/ Logistics	Time
England in the 18th Century	Introduce topic			
	Prepare class to watch video *David Copperfield*	Review questions for follow-up discusion	Handouts #6–1, 2 Video SA-24 (28 min.) VCR, TV monitor	40 minutes
	Show video	Watch video Take notes mentally		
Industry, power, trans-portation; Effects on British society	Prepare class for assigned student presentations next week			10 minutes
		Homework: Answer ques-tions about video. Review history text, pp. 156–168; and science text, pp. 243–248 (technologies)		
(Small-Group Follow-Up)	Set up discussion groups; appoint student recorder in each group to summarize		Groups of eight seated in circles Aides assigned to coordinate Flipchart/pen for each group	
	Aide monitors discussion	Discuss responses to review questions on Dickens video; recorder takes notes		
	Gather groups to report	Recorders report to whole class		
	Guide discussion to conclusions	Tape sheets to wall		40 minutes

CHAPTER 12

Testing Learning Achievement and Student Competencies

▶ *To what previous planning element should tests for student learning directly relate?*

▶ *What can be the forms for tests and other measures of learning?*

▶ *How can themes and student project results be judged?*

▶ *How can student portfolios be assessed?*

▶ *What relation should standardized testing have to this systematic planning process?*

▶ *What are five phases in the evaluation of learning?*

Subject-content and learning objectives lead to instructional procedures for accomplishing the objectives. Now we turn to testing instruments for evaluating student learning. The evaluation component of systematic planning recognizes the direct relationship between learning objectives and test items. A student should anticipate being tested in the same type of performance indicated by the objectives. The verb component of the objective specifies the form that a test item should take:

- **identify or recognize:** choosing an answer in an objective-type test item

- **list or label:** writing a word or brief statement

- **state or describe:** speaking or writing a short or lengthy answer

- **solve or calculate:** choosing a solution or calculating a numerical answer

- **compare or differentiate:** writing about a relationship or choosing an answer that shows a relationship

- **operate or construct:** rating the quality of performance or product against preset criteria

- **formulate or organize:** writing a plan or choosing an order of items relative to a plan

- **predict or judge:** writing a description of what is expected to happen, or choosing from alternative solutions

- **develop or create:** using a checklist or rating scale to judge the result of both a process and its product

In the testing and measurement area, this relationship between action verb and test item is an indication of the validity of the test question. When a number of test items for a specific objective (for multiple testing needs) have the same student learning results, then the test items are considered reliable.

MEASURING LEARNING IN FOUR DOMAINS

Here is a review of testing instruments appropriate for the learning domains introduced under "Subject Content" and "Learning Objectives" (see pages 41–46). While educators are familiar and experienced with most of these techniques, there are some that may be new to the reader.

Cognitive learning (knowledge)

- Objective-type tests: An advantage of objective-type tests is ease of grading them. A disadvantage is that most frequently they measure only low-level, recall-type objectives. But with careful thought, higher-level cognitive objectives can be treated, especially in multiple-choice items.

  —multiple-choice items

  —true-false items

  —matching items

- Written-answer tests: Another major limitation of objective-type tests is that they do not require students to plan answers and express them in their own words. Written-answer tests overcome this shortcoming, allowing higher-level cognitive objectives to be satisfactorily evaluated.

  —short-answer items

  —essay items

For guidance in preparing objective-type and written-answer test questions, see McBeath in "References and Sources," Section H, page 167, and the books in Section J, page 168.

Psychomotor learning (performance skills)

By using a performance test, you determine how well a student can carry out a particular task. Both the process and the quality of a resulting product can be evaluated.

- Evaluate the performance procedure with a **checklist** containing sequential steps that are checked off as the student correctly carries out the actions.

- To judge the quality of the resulting product, use a **rating scale** consisting of a list of criteria rated on a scale with three to five levels from low to high.

See an example of a checklist and a rating scale in Appendix A on page 118. Another rating scale for student presentations that includes teacher comments is shown on page 160 of Appendix B.

Affective and interpersonal behaviors (attitudes and relationships)

Just as it is difficult to write affective-domain objectives, it takes careful thought to assess the degree to which students accomplish these objectives. Attitudes can be inferred indirectly only through a student's words and observable performance. The common methods for gathering data about affective and interpersonal objectives are:

- questionnaires or rating scales completed by students to indicate their feelings, values, and beliefs

- observations of student behavior while at work

- interviews in which students are asked specific questions by an interviewer (preferably a person not directly affiliated with the instructional program), or by talking with teachers, aides, and other students about the subject student

For further practical information on testing methods, refer to Chapter 5 in Murphy and Schiller, cited in "References and Sources," Section B, page 165.

ASSESSING THEME AND PROJECT RESULTS

When interdisciplinary themes and group or individual projects become important aspects of an instructional program, careful thought needs to be given to how to evaluate student learning results. Besides acquiring factual knowledge, individuals or students working in groups should demonstrate creative talents, organizational skills, problem-solving ability, and other higher-order process competencies and accomplishments. Measuring these performance results requires instruments other than conventional paper-and-pencil tests. In terms of the content objectives, while planning a unit (and probably during its implementation, because things can change), the teaching team needs to decide on the criteria to judge successful learning. Such questions as the following might be asked: How well does each student . . .

- fulfill agreed individual activities, with assessment of strengths and weaknesses?

- function as a member of the group?

- handle his or her responsibilities?

- exhibit knowledge of the subject content?

- organize ideas and content?

- show initiative and originality?

- exhibit leadership ability?

- use the knowledge learned in applications, inferences, etc.?

- express himself or herself in writing?

- communicate verbally?

- participate in the final oral or written report for the project?

The teacher and possibly other students in a group can use a rating scale to assess each student's level of accomplishment for each criterion, based on each his or her responsibilities and participation.

ASSESSING STUDENT PORTFOLIOS AND REPORTS

The suggestion to use portfolios and student diaries or activity logs was made on page 58, under the "Student-Prepared Materials" heading. Now use a rating scale to judge the quality of each student's submitted material on the bases of:

- purposes served

- content organization

- attractiveness of the portfolio, journal, or report

- unusual or creative features

- quantity of materials

- quality of written materials (organization, grammar and usage, neatness)

- quality of visual materials (artwork, image composition, continuity, clear communication)

By reviewing the content of a portfolio, diary, or log, the teacher can make objective judgments of a student's intellectual growth and skills development over a period of time.

PHASES IN EVALUATION OF LEARNING

Measuring learning is important at various points during implementation of an instructional program.

Pretest

Before starting an instructional unit, determining the level of student preparation can be useful. Although no grading is involved, pretest questions can indicate whether students have the prerequisite knowledge and skills necessary for starting to study a topic. (For example, does the student have basic math competencies before starting to study algebra problems?) Also, by testing for topic content, you can determine if a student may already have achieved some of the objectives to be studied. (If so, he or she could skip ahead rather than restudying that content.)

The pretest can most easily be prepared at the time the post-test for a topic is being developed (see next page). Representative questions selected from the post-test can be adapted or rewritten for the pretest, along with other prerequisite content questions. Although the pretest may be developed near the end of a planning cycle, it is used prior to or at the beginning of the topical instructional period.

Use the results of the pretest as guidance for any necessary preparatory learning, often by a student successfully completing remedial self-study modules. Also, possibly permit advanced students to skip some or all basic content in the new topic, allowing them to study the topic in more depth, or to engage in other supplemental or chosen work.

While pretesting may not be appropriate for every topic in an instructional program, it can provide the following benefits:

- It determines readiness for a topic by alerting the student and the teacher to what each student does and does not already know about the topic.

- It indicates the point at which each student can best start the topic, or the need to complete prerequisite content before studying the new topic.

- It may motivate students to study the topic because, as they read pretest questions, their curiosity and interest may be aroused.

- It indicates the style and methods of testing that will be used in evaluation of learning.

- It enables the teacher to organize and schedule instruction to avoid wasting time on things already known, and thus plan for maximum efficiency in terms of instruction and use of learning time.

- It provides base data for determining student growth in learning through comparison of scores on pre- and post-tests (see the example in Figure 10 on page 85).

- It indicates potential groupings for students, such as supportive groups in which one student can assist another to overcome deficiencies, or advanced groups in which more developed skills would be applied.

- It provides information useful to the teacher in modifying parts of the program (adding or eliminating objectives and/or activities) so in the future the program can be started at the point that best suits student readiness.

(A topic related to pretesting is "Student Learning Needs" in Chapter 6. Also see pages 134–135 in Appendix B for an example of pretest questions in basic subjects, and page 138 for student profiles of pretest results.)

Consider the students in your program. Based on the foregoing, what information do you want to obtain about them? How would you go about gathering the data? Whose assistance might you request? Then, what use would be made of the results?

Student self-evaluation

As instruction and study proceed, it is important to provide feedback to each student on how well he or she is learning. This can be accomplished by making available short tests, covering key objectives, near the conclusion of a learning sequence. Allow the student to check his or her own answers. By completing such self-check tests, a student can evaluate his or her progress, recognize difficulties or confusion in understanding, and review material prior to taking the teacher's test covering the same objectives. This procedure can better ensure student preparation for and success in the evaluation for the topic.

This is another good example of how our planning process serves the "doing things *with* students" concept for satisfactory learning that is important in Stage 3 of the McBeath model of educational change (Figure 1 on page 9).

Post-test or other final evaluation

It is standard procedure to evaluate student learning for a topic or unit of study, either at a predetermined time or, with flexible learning, when the student or group is ready to be tested. Depending on the goal, objectives, and activities, accomplishments can be measured by a written test, a performance evaluation, a project display and/or report (written or oral), or other specific-outcome evidence. It is beneficial for students to experience judging each other's projects and participation activities.

If it is in keeping with the mission of the school for students to master the content of a topic or theme, then students should be given an opportunity to remediate any learning deficiency revealed on a test. Thus, it may be necessary to develop multiple forms of written tests to allow for student retesting after restudy in order to have more than one opportunity to reach competencies specified by the learning objectives.

The results of student learning should be recorded in a notebook or with a software spreadsheet program. Also, students can maintain a record of their own accomplishments and progress. When engaging in sequences of self-directed module study, each student can be provided with a course map or module flow sequence showing topics or units assigned or otherwise agreed upon for study (see Figure 8). As each one is satisfied, the student can check it off or obtain a signature of approval from the teacher. A visual reference provides each student with an ongoing view of his or her own progress and can be beneficial when shared with parents.

FIGURE 8
A Map of Modules for Self-Directed Learning

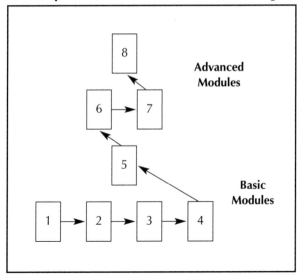

Formative (tryout) evaluation

In any restructured program, we strive for a high level of successful student learning. Therefore, as the program (or a portion of it) becomes ready for initial use, why not do a test run to determine how well it can do the job for which it has been designed? This can be done either with a small group of students (possibly during a summer school program) or on a large scale (a full semester or school year) for the first time. A test run, called *formative evaluation,* answers the question, "How are we doing?" It can determine

weaknesses in the instructional plan and show how students are progressing during instruction so that modifications and improvements can be made before full implementation or subsequent uses to ensure a better level of ongoing success.

Formative evaluation can be based on:

- observations of students at work
- test results
- partial portfolio completions
- verbal reactions offered by students
- suggestions from colleagues, assistants, and other project participants

The results of this evaluation relate not only to the suitability of the objectives, subject content, learning methods, and materials for presentations, group activities, and self-directed study modules, but also to the roles of personnel, the use of facilities, equipment, materials, and time schedules that can affect student performance for achieving the objectives and the original mission goals.

Questions like these might be used to gather data for formative evaluation:

- Do the self-evaluation tests and the post-test satisfactorily measure the learning objectives?
- In terms of the objectives for the topic, is learning at an acceptable level? (For example, if 76 percent of students accomplish 80 percent of the objectives, is this acceptable, based on standards indicated in the mission goals?)
- Where are any weaknesses noted that should be revised for improved learning?
- Are students able to use the knowledge or perform the skills at an acceptable level?
- Were attitudes positively affected?
- How long a time period did the instruction and learning require? Is this acceptable?
- Did the activities seem appropriate and manageable to the teachers and students?
- Were the materials convenient and easy to locate, handle, use, and file?

- Are records of student progress and other program matters convenient to collect, maintain, and report?

- What were the students' reactions to the methods of study, to the activities, to the materials used, and to the evaluation methods?

- What reactions do teachers, assistants, the administrator, parents, and community persons have to the program's content and operation?

- What overall or specific revisions in the program seem necessary?

- What improvements are being made?

The answers to these questions can be used not only to make positive changes, but also to inform interested persons about the present status of the program. (See the formative evaluation questions for the new program example on page 151 in Appendix B.)

In the event that major revisions in the program become necessary, then one or more repeated tryouts should be held until you are satisfied that results are approaching what has been anticipated with an acceptable degree of success.

Summative evaluation

Finally, the results of the new program should be determined and reported each time it is implemented (probably yearly). This is the summative evaluation that can identify potential program improvement needs each time the instruction is conducted. (See procedures in Chapter 13 that treat the summative evaluation topic.)

STANDARDS OF ACHIEVEMENT

There is much discussion about the increasing emphasis on using statewide standardized tests to measure student achievement and even teacher performance. While this procedure has the ring of sound accountability, questions should be raised about the effects of this requirement.

Effects of standardized tests

When used in proper context, standardized tests have a place in measuring student learning for essential grade-level reading, writing, and mathematical concept requirements in all schools. In other academic subjects, standardized tests, as a simplistic attempt to encourage educational reform, may not relate directly to what is being taught in many schools. As one high school student stated in an interview, "These tests don't really show our understanding of the materials we're taught." True accountability requires direct measurements for the learning objectives in all school courses.

Ask yourself these questions when judging the impact of standardized testing:

- Do the pressures of such tests tend to control and narrow the curriculum that is taught, so that "teaching for the test" becomes more important than other curricula needs and time spent in more important teaching/learning activities?

- Does this emphasis detract from students' creativity, forcing them just to memorize information and search only for the "right answer" in subject content on multiple-choice or similar tests (convergent-type thinking as in Stage 1 of the McBeath model in Figure 1 on page 9)?

- Do teachers change their teaching methods to do a better job, or is it more drill and study without a broad learning perspective that leads to student understandings of practical applications of the concepts and principles on which test items are based?

The hope is that requiring standardized testing will improve learning and help students to attain a more effective education. Testing by itself does not change the instructional process. Beyond scoring well on the immediate tests, what are the long-term learning benefits for performance in the real world? Standardized tests can be just another band-aid solution for improvement. And there is evidence that in some school systems, when sufficient numbers of students do not attain a desired standard, the required standard is lowered so more of them can pass.

Recall how learning objectives can be related to statewide standards in academic subjects (see page 45), and then can be accomplished through appropriate teaching/learning activities. There is really no easy escape from fully transforming the system. This is a fair and equitable way of leading to and determining educational results. If carefully applied, the design process described here can prepare students to show positive results on standardized tests, as well as in other important educational outcomes. (Refer to the components of summative evaluation in Chapter 13 for what should be included in a comprehensive method of evaluating an educational program's effectiveness. For further consideration of standardized testing, refer to Kohn in "References and Sources," Section J, page 168.)

MEASURING ACHIEVEMENT

In most conventional educational programs, the performance of one student is compared to that of other students in the class. A test based on relative standards would indicate that one student has learned more or less than have others. The result is a relative or normative rating of each student within the group (for example, percentile standing with letter grades: 10 percent receive A; 20 percent, B; 50 percent, C; 20 percent, D; and 10 percent, F, as shown on a bell-shaped curve). The rating does not necessarily signify the level of proficiency of any learner in the group with respect to a specific standard of accomplishment indicated by learning objectives. This method does not fit a plan in which we should strive to make instruction and the resulting learning effective and successful for the great majority of students in a class.

The specific standard of accomplishment is the *performance* or *criterion* specified by each learning objective. "Criterion-referenced testing" measures how well each student attains the required level of comprehension and competence specified for the objectives pursued. As stated previously, the anticipated goal is to guide each student to best achieve his or her learning objectives, even if this requires restudy and retesting. Some students may strive to attain higher performance levels or even higher-level learning objectives. With this approach, study time often becomes a variable while students strive to reach the standards specified by their learning objectives. A

student's final level of achievement is not dependent on the performance of other students.

The terms "competency-based instruction" and "mastery learning" are also used to signify a program that provides successful learning experiences for the great majority of students. This goal is in part the justification for giving increased attention to self-directed learning methods for some groups of content objectives, providing more than a single opportunity for a student who does not reach competency the first time to restudy, receive tutorial or other assistance, self-test, and then be retested to measure learning until the mastery level is attained.

▶ *Can you relate the two standards of achievement (normative rating and criterion-referenced) to stages within the McBeath model of educational change (shown in Figure 1 on page 9)?*

▶ *Do you accept the criterion-referenced standard for learning as essential in education today?*

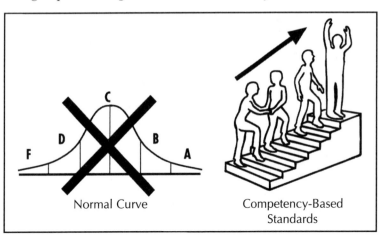

Normal Curve   Competency-Based Standards

GRADING STUDENTS

As each student satisfies the assigned or agreed-upon learning objectives at the required or accepted achievement levels, some form of acknowledgment of those accomplishments should be made, preferably other than the traditional letter-grade report card. As explained in the consideration of learning objectives on page 43, two levels of accomplishment may be specified: a minimum satisfactory level, or a superior level. Grading results can take the form of progress reports that reflect student achievement, growth, and even attitudes. It may be acceptable to use a numerical system. A scale like this could be developed:

- Level 1: unsatisfactory, requires extensive restudy

- Level 2: some improvements are essential

- Level 3: satisfactory results

- Level 4: superior accomplishments

In addition to assessments of a student's success in satisfying performance standards in academic subjects, interdisciplinary themes, and projects, assessments of the student's affective behaviors may also be included. Under such headings as *collaboration, re-sponsibility, self-direction,* and *problem solving,* teachers can write comments such as:

- "increased cooperative level within groups"

- "more positive attitude toward reading"

- "approaches problems more analytically"

- "sets her own schedule and now follows through much better"

To reemphasize—when he or she does not attain the accepted numerical standard, a student should have the opportunity to restudy, be coached or tutored as necessary, and be retested or otherwise re-evaluated until reaching at least minimum mastery. ◆

CHAPTER 13

Summative Evaluation: Assessing Program Results and Extending the Program

▶ *How can you decide whether systematic instructional planning can result in an effective new program?*

▶ *For what program outcomes should evidence be gathered?*

▶ *How can the effectiveness and efficiency of a new program be evaluated?*

▶ *How can continuing program expenses be determined?*

▶ *How can you gather reactions to the program once it is fully implemented?*

▶ *What long-term benefits could be anticipated, and how can information about them be obtained?*

▶ *How can the results of program outcomes be disseminated?*

As noted in "Standards of Achievement" (page 80), the major benefits of public education programs often are measured through statewide and national standardized tests. It is expected that students should reach acceptable standards. Their accomplishment of an agreed level usually is a key indication of an educational program's success.

In the design plan presented here, measurements of a new program's merits should go beyond the results of standardized tests. Summative evaluation is a continuous process that determines the degree to which a number of major outcomes are attained by the end of an instructional program period, along with any need for improvement. The following categories of outcomes need evaluation in terms of the program's identified needs (Chapter 6) and mission goals (pages 35–36):

- effectiveness of student learning

- efficiency of the program

- continuing program expenses

- reactions to the program by students, parents, and others involved

- long-term benefits of the program in terms of changes stated in the mission goals

- successful extension of the program within the school or in the district

Why do we need to perform such a comprehensive final evaluation? Isn't it enough just to determine student learning levels? If they are satisfactory, isn't that sufficient proof that the program is successful?

The systematic plan we have been applying would be incomplete unless we fulfill this final step of summative evaluation. This provides for full accountability; by gathering such evidence, not only can program results be determined, but the need for ongoing program improvements can also be identified. When you purchase a new automobile, you expect it will give good service for how long . . . five to ten years? You have it checked periodically and correct shortcomings to be certain you will get your "money's worth" for the desired length of time. The same is true for a transformed or new educational program. The need now is to determine the degree to which the major outcomes are being attained. Over time, it is likely that the characteristics of students and program goals may change. Revisions may be necessary if continuous success is to be achieved.

Consider who would be the best person or team to handle this summative evaluation. It should be conducted by an impartial person or group. Individuals directly engaged in the program may be biased and may not objectively gather evidence and reach valid conclusions. Possibly teachers not involved in the program, others from the school district office, or a faculty member along with graduate students from a nearby university school of education could conduct this evaluation. Selection of the person or persons to handle this summative evaluation should be made during early program development. This would allow for necessary planning, decisions about which data to collect, and progress documentation to be obtained as the program is implemented each time.

EFFECTIVENESS OF STUDENT LEARNING

A question to ask is, *"To what degree did students achieve competency with the learning objectives?"* This is the measure of program effectiveness. Based on the learning objectives for subject topics, themes, self-directed student learning modules, and small-group project activities—and then the tests, performance ratings, and other evaluation methods—accomplishment of the objectives can be determined.

The data collected from these appraisals provide answers to the above question. By calculation or using a statistical software program, accomplishment of objectives can be determined. A sample summary in tabular form is shown in Figure 9.

For each curriculum area and other aspects of the new program, numerical results can be determined. For the six students in Figure 9, 90 percent of the objectives were satisfied. With a result like this, we have a measure of instructional effectiveness. Based on the original mission goals, a decision can be made to accept the results or to take corrective actions. (Note that question 11 received only one correct answer. This may be an invalid test question and should be examined.)

Another aspect of effectiveness in learning is to determine the gain in scores between pretesting and post-testing. This relationship is illustrated in Figure 10. Note the large gains for objectives 1, 5, and 7, while small improvements occurred for objectives 2 and 9, but the overall evidence of learning is strong.

See Appendix A for examples of evaluations of learning effectiveness.

EFFICIENCY OF THE PROGRAM

Educational efficiency can refer to how well the program arranges and manages the use of personnel time, facilities, and funds. Indications of time spent by teachers in instruction and counseling students, student study time to achieve topical objectives, amount of time that various facilities are in use, and monetary expenses calculated on a per-student basis can all provide measures of efficiency.

It may not always be convenient or practical to record such data. An alternative is to consider the

(Continued on page 86)

FIGURE 9
An Analysis of Test Questions Measuring Cognitive Objectives

A. Unit Objectives	Test Questions
A.	2, 4, 11
B.	1, 7
C.	3, 5, 12
D.	8, 10
E.	5, 9

B. Student	Correct Answers to Questions											
	1	2	3	4	5	6	7	8	9	10	11	12
AJ	x	x	x	x		x	x	x	x	x	x	x
SF	x	x	x	x		x		x				
TY	x	x	x	x	x	x	x	x	x	x		x
LM	x	x	x	x	x	x	x	x	x	x		x
RW	x	x	x	x	x	x	x	x	x	x		x
WB	x		x	x	x	x	x		x	x		x

C. Student	Objectives Satisfied				
	A	B	C	D	E
AJ	x	x	x	x	
SF	x	x	x	x	
TY	x	x	x	x	x
LM	x	x	x	x	x
RW	x	x	x	x	x
WB	x		x	x	

FIGURE 10
Using Pretest and Post-Test Results to Determine Learning Improvements

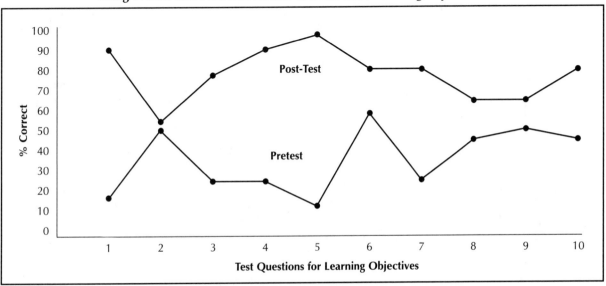

number of students in the program, the variety of teaching/learning activities, and the degree of learning effectiveness as indications of program efficiency; then compare with conventional instructional methods and their results to obtain an indication of efficiency for the new program.

CONTINUING PROGRAM EXPENSES

Another important outcome is to determine what the program is costing to operate. Although a school is not the same as a business operation, specific factors affecting costs can be determined, and their acceptability can be judged. Under the "Budget" heading for logistics and support services in Chapter 11, there is a list of items for developmental costs; operating costs are listed on pages 64–65. By calculating the annual recurring operational costs (plus any expenses for revising and updating parts of the program), you have an indication of it what costs to operate the program. As with the efficiency outcome category, the administration and faculty should decide if this is reasonable and acceptable, often in terms of the program's effectiveness and efficiency levels. If the cost is not acceptable, decide what modifications should be made in the program for savings or to provide more efficient uses for resources.

(See pages 119–120 in Appendix A for an example of program expenses.)

REACTIONS TO THE PROGRAM

During the tryout phase, after program development, opinions about the new program should have been obtained from students, teachers, parents, and other persons affiliated with the program. This is part of formative evaluation. The opinions helped you judge what changes should be made. Now, with the program in operation, it's important to obtain further reactions from a broad selection of involved persons.

First, identify individuals who have had a direct relationship with the program or in other important ways are affected by it. Second, decide how they should be approached for their reactions. These two methods can be used to gather information:

- Questionnaires that ask about the content and activities of the program, student relations with

each other and with teachers and staff, and direct benefits to other persons involved in the program. The questionnaire can consist of checklists, rating scales, and open-ended questions for written responses.

- Interviews with randomly selected participants, to include more personalized versions of the items indicated above. This is a more difficult and time-consuming procedure, but could be used beneficially with a few persons from each participation category.

These reactions should be obtained during and at the conclusion of the academic year. At those times, details about the program should still be fresh in mind, and the persons to be contacted are nearby or otherwise convenient to reach.

(For examples of questions to ask various groups for evaluating a new program, see page 120 in Appendix A.)

LONG-TERM BENEFITS

Program outcomes beyond the immediate results (test scores)—time spent in the program, costs, facilities use, and immediate reactions—also need examination. No doubt many mission goals can be assessed only after instruction is concluded and students have progressed to the next phase of their education, or from high school to the outside world.

This can be a complex phase of summative evaluation because many important results, such as attitudes, are in the affective domain. While outcomes such as the number of students performing at grade level or changes in the school drop-out or disciplinary rates are easy to quantify in subsequent years, other outcomes may be more difficult to clearly identify and measure. How can you determine students' fulfillment of roles as good citizens? The degree to which former students are law abiding, vote in local, state, and federal elections, and participate in other social and civic matters can be positive citizenship indicators, but may not be evident for many years.

Some commonly used methods to gather evidence of long-term benefits are:

- Examining records to check grades, reported activities, and following-year anecdotal entries about students, as found in school files, to ascertain how they are now performing in classes.

- Conducting interviews with students who have been in the new program, with teachers they have in following years, with parents, with community persons having contact with students from the program, and with former students now employed in the community. These interviews can reveal students' present competencies and behaviors resulting in part from their participation in the new program.

- Compiling questionnaires, which can be a substitute for interviews.

Hopefully, as based on the mission goals, the results will show that students:

- exhibit positive attitudes and a level of enthusiasm toward their learning experiences

- have acquired information, intellectual abilities, and performance skills that equip them to successfully pursue further education

- can apply what they have learned in chosen vocational endeavors

Gather further evidence of the program's effects by determining:

- the increase in parental involvement in the school

- the number and quality of volunteers providing services in the school

- partnerships developed with community groups

- general attitudes expressed toward the school in the local media and through other outlets

EXTENSION OF THE NEW PROGRAM

A key principle of this school restructuring plan is to start small, with a few concerned and motivated teachers who, with encouragement and guidance, can design, develop, and implement the innovative program, evaluating and improving as they proceed; then to expand the program gradually to include other teaching teams and classes of students. The manner and degree to which this expansion takes place in the school is an important aspect of transformational success.

The complete restructuring of a school program may take four years or more. Therefore, an examination of this category in summative evaluation may not be of value until a few years after the program has been implemented. But even after a year or so, there should be some evidence of progress in the school to provide a level of success in terms of the vision and mission, and an interest and action for expanding beyond the initial participatory group. If this extension does not happen within a reasonable time, the program could decline and even terminate with the school returning to traditional Stage 1 principles, practices, and outcomes in the McBeath model (Figure 1 on page 9).

REPORTING RESULTS

From both public relations and accountability positions, the results of summative evaluation should be widely reported. This can be done as a presentation to involved and interested persons and groups, and as a printed report for distribution and release to the news and television media.

Future support for the program, including assistance with program expansion, can be affected by this report.

Try to collect data on each of the six parts of summative evaluation described in this chapter. Then analyze the levels on which that data answer the school needs and student learning needs (Chapter 6) that initially served to create the new program. Enumerate how the vision statement and mission goals (see pages 35–36) are being accomplished. It may be difficult to show direct results for all goals immediately because a number of them cannot be realized until the students are beyond their school days. But over a period of years, there can be some indications of all accomplishments.

If one or more presentations are to be made, consider the audience and its members' interests. Use data in graphic form on slides or overhead transparencies (preferably attractively computer-generated), and encourage responses and questions. Consider showing brief program activity examples on videotape, and even having students make presentations that describe and display their work. Be sure that all involved teachers participate. Include or recognize parents, community persons, older students, university personnel, and others who assisted in the process. Utilize services of local media to distribute results within the community.

For a printed report, follow these suggestions:

- Give the report an interesting title.

- Summarize highlights or important results, so they can be grasped quickly (such as in an Executive Summary).

- Describe supporting data with graphics.

- Do not become too detailed or use technically worded statistics.

- Refer to persons who can supply more information.

- Conclude by noting appropriate recommendations that have been made for continuing, modifying, and/or extending the program.

A Web page might be designed to further publicize the new program and invite interest.

If you are involved in designing a new or transformed program, you may have already decided on some of the matters that should receive attention in summative evaluation. Prepare to act on them as your program attains full-scale implementation. See "References and Sources," Section K, on page 168 for more in-depth treatment of summative evaluation components. ◆

CHAPTER 14

Guiding toward Success

▶ *What concerns need consideration when initiating a new program?*

▶ *What matters need attention when implementing the program?*

▶ *What practices can ensure continuing success?*

Chapter 1 raised a slogan for educational change: *It's a new plan for instruction we need, my friends!* This guidebook has built on this statement by examining six essential components of systematic instructional planning and project management: *analysis, initiation, development, implementation, evaluation,* and *extension.* These components are treated within the context of Stage 3 in the McBeath model of educational change (see Figure 1 on page 9). As we conclude our exploration, the three introductory questions above can help the reader to review and strengthen understandings and actions relative to the school transformational process.

INITIATING THE NEW PROGRAM

By now you have faced the reality that the planning process presented here requires careful thought for the many interdependent components to produce positive learning results. When you first start planning, it may seem overwhelming, not entirely necessary, and maybe even discouraging. Hopefully, your planning team has been guided and assisted to recognize and understand the merits of this approach and the benefits that can result from attention to precise details.

Sometimes when an educator is first introduced to this process, or sees the listing of the 16 essential process questions (pages 16–17), the reaction is, "Doesn't this approach discourage creativity in teaching? And isn't this a mechanistic, rather than a humanistic method of instructional planning?" Here are responses to these questions:

If **creativity** means formulating, developing, and expressing new ideas and original thoughts as ways to solve problems, then this process certainly allows for creativity. Numerous opportunities are available for collaborating with other educators and expressing one's own ideas and independent thinking in unique ways. The process is flexible, as planning elements can be developed in any order, while being closely related.

A **humanistic** method of instruction is one that recognizes the individual learner in terms of his or her own capabilities, individual differences, present ability levels, interests, and attitudes. Elements of the process

(Continued on page 90)

> include an examination of student charac-
> teristics and identification of readiness
> levels for learning. Furthermore, the imple-
> mentation of systematic planning provides
> variety in instruction, including self-directed
> and small-group interactive learning to build
> individual self-esteem and communication
> skills. All of these features contribute to a
> more humanistic approach than do passive
> and rote learning.
>
> —From Kemp, *The Instructional Design Process*
> (see "References and Sources," Section E, page 166).

When a new program is being considered and planned, a number of suggestions can be applied that directly contribute to potential success:

- Judge the human-performance capabilities of teachers who will participate in terms of each individual's personal beliefs, expectations, motivation level, and commitment to strive toward successful change.

- Offer to provide teachers with incentives and recognition for their positive efforts. These may include release from certain routine duties, professional training, support with new equipment and services, opportunities to attend conferences and special meetings, and even merit pay.

- Early on, after initial plans are firm, communicate with any groups that could have potential involvement—other teachers, administrators, parents, community people, and so on. Invite input, reactions, and support. Be patient and open to new ideas. Reach agreements.

- As you build the planning team, help individuals identify and express what personal benefits they could derive from participation. This can help to raise their enthusiasm and motivation levels.

- Guide involved teachers to broaden their knowledge and skills so they may carry out planning with confidence.

- Keep everyone informed as the program develops.

- Recognize that all will not advance smoothly. There will be challenges to face and obstacles to overcome. Deal with problems and disagreements promptly and constructively, while having the confidence to take risks.

- With initial planning, include vision and mission statements. Be specific in terms of the local situation, the needs to be served, and the nature of the student population and the community.

- Set a realistic time frame, and be flexible but still firm on meeting agreed deadlines and having individuals fulfill their responsibilities.

- Use effective group-process skills—respect individuals, encourage input and participation, request worthwhile contributions, and acknowledge good work. All will lead to satisfaction and the desire to continue or extend contributions.

- Access information sources to find out about other innovative projects, similar to your project, for comparable students and communities. Use the key expressions listed on page 27 to guide a search and explore what else might be obtained through the World Wide Web.

- Plan visits to other identified new programs, and question involved teachers, administrators, and even students.

- Recognize and act on the difference between just giving students the opportunities to learn and ensuring that all students, or at least the great majority, do learn successfully.

- Encourage students to get into the spirit of change through their participation, enjoyment, and successful learning.

In addition to the above suggestions, review "Colleagues as Co-Members of the Planning Team" and "Personal Behaviors for Planning" in Chapter 5; and "Personnel Capabilities" in Chapter 11. Although written for organizational change in businesses, many of the factors that Tosti recommends in his article listed in "References and Sources," Section B, on pages 165–166, are appropriate to public education efforts and reinforce what is described here.

DESIGNING AND IMPLEMENTING THE PROGRAM

Evidence shows that it may take three to four years to plan, develop, try out, evaluate, refine, and fully implement phases of a systematically designed new school program. Knowing this, there should be an understanding and commitment to devising and implementing a long-term strategy based on the mission goals developed in the first phase of planning. During this time, the following should be accomplished:

- Carry out the planning stages outlined in previous chapters of this guidebook, or your modifications of them.

- Make use of, or modify, the suggestions on the mechanics of planning (pages 72–73), which can provide an effective method of handling and interrelating all planning components.

- Allow adequate time for all involved to fully develop new skills and positive relationships.

- Build teacher confidence in selecting and using technologies.

- Integrate appropriate technologies into the curriculum plan, and use various media to foster communication and to improve record keeping (schedules, student progress, records and reports, budget and expense categories, inventories of materials for use, locations of equipment for teacher and student use, and so forth).

- Recognize the benefits of developing a comprehensive school technology program as described on pages 59–60.

- Periodically examine and critically evaluate all components of the new program as you proceed, and revise them as obstacles or unanticipated circumstances are encountered.

- Try not to get bogged down with minor details that could become a discouragement, leading to making superficial or hasty changes in an instructional program.

- When things go wrong, examine what happened and revise accordingly. Learn from both successes and failures.

- Try to keep up with developments concerning innovative methods and new practices by having the school or district librarian watch for and alert you to educational journal articles, reform newsletters, announcements of meetings and conferences of possible interest, new books, and Internet resources.

Besides keeping parents and caregivers informed about the new program, give particular attention to fostering their involvement as the program progresses. Offer workshops, school fairs, and other activities that involve parents along with their children. In addition to open-house gatherings, teachers should schedule meetings with individual parents to report on their child's progress, difficulties encountered, and suggested home activities to improve student learning. Recall the suggestions offered to interest parents, and the question raised on page 70. There is no simple answer to the question, "In what specific ways might you actively encourage and motivate parents and other adults to become more involved in local school affairs?" Possibly take a survey to determine if Saturday meetings may be preferred to the usual weekday evening times. Consider repeating a workshop to fit parent schedules, or even arranging to use a school bus to conveniently transport parents who do not have other transportation.

Also initiate a plan to encourage older adults (often senior citizens) to become school volunteers. Their experiences and interests can provide many useful services to both teachers and students. (See the publication *Becoming a School Partner: A Guidebook for Organizing Intergenerational Partnerships in Schools* in "References and Sources," Section L, page 168.)

EVALUATING AND MANAGING THE PROGRAM

In Chapter 11, "Instructional Logistics and Program Support," under the section "Personnel Capabilities" (pages 67–68), leadership and management responsibilities for the program coordinator are listed. Review them, as what follows here serves to supplement those activities and recommendations.

- Establish a plan to objectively monitor student learning and program progress.

- Set benchmarks for the planning team to use in responding to the following formative evaluation questions:

  —Which program components are doing well?

  —Which program components need special attention?

  —What reactions are we getting from students, parents, and other program participants?

- Do not expect all students to succeed immediately. Recognize their differences and gradually guide them to success. Note again the 90 to 95 percent achievement level that should be strived for.

- Prepare and present progress reports to district administrators, other teachers, parents, community groups, and other interested persons.

- Develop a close relationship with the district administration to establish a strong site-based management protocol relating to policies, practices, and support for new program needs.

- Build and maintain trust, a sharing attitude, continuing support, and accountability among all participants.

- Identify other teachers who may be ready to participate in program expansion.

- Coordinate with other school activities and innovative efforts in the school to which the new program should be linked.

- Check how available funds can be reallocated or additional resources acquired to support the program.

- Work with district financial personnel to move the new program from soft to hard money categories within the school budget.

- Establish a student code of behavior so as to maintain a safe and orderly school environment that is conducive to teaching and learning. For a list of practical items to include in a student code of behavior, see Murphy and Schiller's *Transforming America's Schools* ("References and Sources," Section B, page 165).

- Follow district policy (or suggest changes in keeping with new roles teachers must fulfill) for evaluating the skills, performance, and accomplishments of teachers involved in the project.

- Recognize the school principal's role as a guide and facilitator, rather than the controlling authority who gives directions and makes the important school decisions.

- Extend the new or restructured program to involve other "ready" teachers and classes of students until the whole school is transformed.

- Coordinate with feed-in and feed-to schools to correlate curricula offerings with student preparation to provide for the smooth transition of students.

- Invite higher education personnel to become involved in program phases—development, implementation, and evaluation. Both professors and college students may be "volunteer" participants, a cost-saving advantage.

- Try to share your new program philosophy, activities, and results with education professors so that you may have influence on restructuring the teacher education program.

TRANSFORMATION CAN WORK *IF . . .*

Finally, if you can stand back and objectively view all that we have been examining with respect to the educational transformation process, you will see that a number of beliefs and practices are necessary to attain successful systemic change. Here is a review and extension of key suggestions offered:

- Strong administrative understanding and support with sufficient initial and ongoing financial resources from a number of sources.

- A commitment to school-based management and decision making with teachers fully involved.

- A shift in the teachers' belief structure from an authoritarian, teacher-centered classroom role to a democratic, inquiry-centered one that is typified by doing things *with* students (Stage 3 of the McBeath model, Figure 1 on page 9).

- The acceptance of a systematic process of instructional planning, with detailed attention to all necessary components.

- An instructional designer, well qualified in innovative educational practices and knowledgeable about the systematic process of instructional planning, who guides and supports those involved in the transformational efforts.

- A variety of learning experiences for students that may include class presentations, group activities, and self-directed learning.

- The extensive use of various technologies to provide the variety of learning experiences necessary for students.

- Close cooperation among teachers, administrators, parents, community persons, and local agencies.

Be aware that for some individuals, the initial enthusiasm for a new endeavor can weaken and fade in time. The excitement of creation and mental challenge could subside, and for some teachers, the program may appear to become too routine and repetitive. Also, there may be new, more attractive events that could shift a person's interests. But even in view of this possible eventuality for some individuals, recognize that attention to three stages of personal involvement of teachers in innovative activities can best ensure their success and continued positive involvement.

- **Readiness**—Identify those persons (teachers, administrators, parents, and others) who are dissatisfied with the present beliefs, practices, and outcomes of education, and in particular their own programs, and who may express an interest in wanting to do things differently to improve student learning and attitudes.

- **Support**—Initiate and continue to guide, assist, and provide resources or otherwise support the efforts of those "ready" to change in a systematic manner.

- **Success**—Results can be personal satisfaction for accomplishments, with reinforcement and motivation to continue and extend the transformational efforts toward further success.

If you have not already read the two following appendices, consider doing so now. They show how the content you have acquired in this guidebook can be developed and implemented. It can work! ◆

APPENDIX A

A School Changes

A description of how a hypothetical middle school starts to transform its instructional program to meet the needs of its students in the Information Age

CHAPTER 15

Starting the Change Process

Stoneridge Middle School (grades 6 through 8) is located in a multiracial neighborhood. The school was built in 1978 and serves 850 students with 30 teachers.

Like other schools today, Stoneridge is facing many unsatisfactory conditions:

- Many student grades on standardized tests are below acceptable levels.

- Too many students express boredom or even negative attitudes toward school and learning itself.

- Reports from the feed-in high school indicate that many students do not have satisfactory preparation in basic subjects.

- There are some conflicts among student racial and ethnic groups.

- Many teachers lack motivation in their teaching.

- Parents show little interest in the school, other than in their own child's accomplishments or deficiencies.

Based on these shortcomings, during a before-school teachers' meeting, the principal, Joan Stefans, presents some thoughts for improving the quality of learning in the school. These include: re-evaluating how basic-skills subjects are taught, doing more with cooperative student group activities, and making greater use of television and computers in classrooms. After hearing this, one teacher states, "We examined our basic-skills teaching a while back, and

tried these technologies before, and it's just more work for us without much happening to students." Another teacher adds, "We need to be stricter in the classroom, assign more homework, and inform parents about difficulties we are having with their children. Kids just don't show the interest in their own education like it was in our day."

It is decided that a committee will be formed to come up with new ideas. After the meeting, some of the teachers discuss the principal's suggestions over lunch. There is little interest, but many agree that changes certainly are necessary in the school.

TEACHERS WHO ARE "READY"

Four teachers are most positive in expressing the need to examine the school's program. Their recognition of limitations within the present program motivates them to explore new ideas. These four—Terry Larson (English), Ruth Lopez (Social Studies), Mark Brown (Mathematics), and Britt Starr (Science)—decide they will offer to be on the committee, and start by sharing thoughts among themselves for changing their teaching.

The four teachers meet with the principal and express a willingness to work on new plans for the school. Principal Stefans agrees to seek funds to reimburse them for some weekend time spent on developing a plan during the next six months. She tells them about innovative programs taking place in some nearby schools. The teachers decide to make visits. Substitute teachers will be assigned to their classes, so they can see the programs in action during the school day.

Over the next few weeks, the teachers visit four middle and junior high schools. They see how a more flexible school-day schedule is used with a variety of group activities and some self-directed learning by individual students. The teachers witness extensive use of computers with effective software, and television in the form of distance learning to help some students with advanced subjects. They also learn how parents and community residents can be encouraged to provide useful assistance to teachers.

The four teachers are impressed and become stimulated with new ideas for making changes, but they are uncertain how to proceed. They ask themselves these questions:

▶ *Where should we start?*

▶ *Should we adopt successful practices we saw?*

▶ *What other nontraditional techniques might we use in our classes?*

▶ *How would we manage changes within our daily schedule?*

▶ *How can we obtain financial help for new materials and equipment?*

▶ *Should experienced teachers from these other schools be asked to advise us?*

There seems to be a number of pieces to consider in order to put things together toward a practical plan for school change. The teachers raise the above questions with Joan Stefans. In reply, she shows them a 1993 report by D. D. Gainey, published by the National Association of Secondary School Principals (NASSP), on school restructuring. (See "References and Sources," Section B, page 165.) It focuses on:

- changing the planning and teaching roles for teachers

- leading and managing responsibilities for administrators in collaborative ways with teachers

- redefining and integrating the school curriculum

- setting flexible schedules for students and teachers

- incorporating new technologies for teaching and learning

- involving parents more actively in school activities

- coordinating human and financial community resources

- measuring learning results in new and detailed ways

The teachers agree with the principal that these concepts could serve as guiding factors within which a new program might be designed for the school.

During this time, Joan is able to observe the four teachers working together. They gradually show increasing enthusiasm and express fresh thoughts about how to make school better for the students. They seem to be sharing ideas very well while developing collaborative relationships. The teachers exhibit a willingness for and an interest in making changes. Their "readiness" can be an important ingredient for getting the change process started, Joan believes.

After weighing all these factors, the principal is prepared to make an important decision: The four teachers will become the experimental group to plan and try out changes in their own teaching. Then, in time, other teachers in the school could become involved.

THE FACILITATOR

The four teachers judge their own abilities for engaging in innovative planning. Each one feels competent in his or her subject area and is comfortable with classroom teaching techniques. But when they consider what they saw during the visits to the other schools and the follow-up questions they had raised, help seems needed. Furthermore, the concepts of school restructuring from the NASSP report that Joan had showed them require other skills beyond their present experiences.

Someone is needed to guide and assist the teachers in planning for the new instructional program, and to help them make decisions in a methodical way. This person should be competent in aspects of the teaching/learning process that may be beyond what the teachers have been trained to do, yet which are essential in educational planning today. These competencies should include the ability to help in:

- **analyzing** present program strengths and weaknesses

- **designing** the goals and objectives for a new program

- **developing** teaching and learning activities, including resources and necessary support

- guiding the **implementation** of the new program

- **evaluating** the learning results and program outcomes

After discussing the need for a facilitator to work with them, the four teachers ask the principal if such a qualified person could be employed as a consultant. Joan Stefans agrees to talk with a couple of education professors she knows at the nearby university, and also to discuss the matter with the school district superintendent. The university professors recommend a colleague in instructional technology who might be interested in the project.

Shortly thereafter, the principal invites the professor to the school. She expresses her desire to get some reform activities started in the middle school, and then she explains that four teachers have proposed to develop a plan for changing their teaching practices to better serve the needs of their students. A person with abilities beyond just curriculum coordination could assist the teachers in developing a new program.

The professor, Randy Lewis, describes his training (undergraduate in chemistry, master's in education, and doctorate in instructional technology) and experience (four years as a high school science teacher, instructional designer for training with a pharmaceutical company for five years, and now a professor for six years).

Ms. Stefans indicates to Dr. Lewis that, with district approval, she would like to hire him as the facilitator for the four teachers. Together they can form a team to examine the school's present instructional program, plan needed changes, and implement the new program.

(In this situation, the facilitator comes from the nearby university. One advantage of this choice is that university students in education may volunteer to help with the development of the new program for the valuable experiences they could acquire. Other potential sources exist for locating a qualified person to fill this important role in the school change process; he or she may come from within the school system, on loan from an instructional development service in a business concern, or as an independent consultant.)

The principal tells the school district superintendent about the project being considered at Stoneridge Middle School. The superintendent is pleased and agrees to present the idea to the school board. With their approval, he indicates, Joan will have control to move ahead with her plan, and reasonable support will be provided as requested. Then a contract could be made to hire Dr. Lewis as consultant.

Once the board has agreed, Ms. Stefans calls Dr. Lewis to advise him of the approval for a consultation agreement, and they decide to meet with the teachers to start their planning.

A DIRECTION FOR CHANGE

When the team meets, the principal sets the stage by recounting the needs that initially served as the stimuli for this project (see page 97). The four teachers express their concerns and what they hope to accomplish with their students. Randy Lewis comments that he is pleased to hear that they have engaged in some preliminary thinking and have a base for change in the needs that were identified. Then he suggests that together they might examine perspectives on new frameworks within which the instructional program could be designed. He starts by raising these questions:

▶ *As compared with the past, what are the differences in our society and in the world today that require changes in our educational programs?*

▶ *How do the changes affect our students now and in preparation for their adult lives?*

▶ *What does all this mean for a middle school instructional program?*

As the principal, teachers, and Randy consider these questions, Randy places on the table a number of publications and encourages the others to browse through them. (See Drucker, Naisbitt and Aburdene, and Toffler in "References and Sources," Section A, page 165; and Perelman, Section B, page 166.) They can help provide a vision of the changes that are necessary for educating our students today.

When they meet a second time, they agree that in today's world, everyone is faced with a bewildering number of alternatives from which decisions must be made. They agree that it is essential for students to develop the abilities to acquire and use complex information, to learn new skills, to assess new situations that can lead to making decisions, to apply creative modes of reasoning, and to solve more difficult problems in order to deal with the unexpected in their lives and to prepare for adult responsibilities.

It is recognized that these goals indicate that what must be taught, and how it should be taught, are now quite different than in the past. These needs require a fundamental rethinking and redesign of instruction to achieve improvements in learning and performance.

At this second meeting, Dr. Lewis builds on the discussion of the broad changes that have been identified. He explains that anyone seriously interested in revising a school program must shift perspective from what is traditionally assumed and practiced concerning the learning process, to new thinking and actions for the emerging Information Age.

For educators to become more aware of the need for this shift from a traditional orientation to a new perspective, Randy introduces a useful model developed by McBeath as a three-stage transformational model of educational change (page 9). By examining the entries for each stage in the model, teachers can identify patterns that comprise beliefs and mindsets that developed in previous societal stages, and now must be rethought for the current Information Age. These patterns—principles, practices, and outcomes—have systematically influenced the key aspects of education. Randy then asks these questions:

▶ *Do you see the rationale for this model today?*

▶ *Can you agree with its structure . . . and the need for teachers to move toward the Stage 3 pattern?*

▶ *Then, if so, what additional entries might you add to Stage 3?*

After discussion and some clarification by Randy, the teachers come up with these additional practices and outcomes for Stage 3:

• Recognize that site-based school management is essential.

• Enhance student motivation by encouraging their active participation in learning.

• Recognize different student learning styles and plan to serve them.

• Provide for more collaborative work by teachers with students, and among students themselves during instruction and learning activities.

• Base much learning on realistic or simulated situations, with meaningful applications of subject content in all curricula areas.

• Assess learning through performance-based measurements, such as portfolio contents.

• Encourage more involvement of parents and the community in the educational program.

• Share responsibility for successful learning among teachers, administrators, students, and parents.

• Provide leadership for continuous improvement in student learning.

The group members agree that many of their present assumptions about students and learning procedures need to be reconsidered. A fresh orientation is necessary, requiring new thinking as to how instruction should be planned, implemented, and evaluated. For systemic change, rather than superficial changes or add-on innovations, systematic redesign of the instructional program becomes essential.

As a summary discussion, the teachers refer to the four school visits they had made earlier. They consider the innovative programs they saw according to their placement within the three stages of the McBeath model. Some programs are just modifying a small part of the school program and could relate to Stage 2, while a few are comprehensive changes, applying many Stage 3 principles, practices, and outcomes. Randy points out that when only one or a few elements of an educational program are changed, there is little overall effect, and in time the reform may be dropped. A total program transformation is necessary in order to lead to successful Stage 3 principles, practices, and outcomes.

Then, to broaden the teachers' perspective even further, Randy takes the four to visit three local businesses that have outstanding Stage 3 training programs. Obviously, the content of a business training program has little direct relationship to a public school program, but the organization, management, support, use of technologies, types of trainee activities, and roles of trainers can provide useful reference points for teachers who wish to make major changes.

Finally, Randy explains that each person has to decide where he or she feels comfortable in the transformational model. After thought and discussion, the teachers agree that the plan they are designing must be directed toward the principles, practices, and outcomes listed for Stage 3. They also recognize that there are some teaching and learning situations in which either Stage 1 or 2 treatment could be appropriate to the requirements and needs or the present orientation of their students.

Understanding these concepts and being able to discuss them with the teachers are two of the reasons why the principal had suggested that a facilitator like Randy Lewis, with his Stage 3 orientation, could successfully guide teachers in changing their educational practices.

NEW PROGRAM PARAMETERS

With the above information and understandings, the principal, teachers, and facilitator agree on the following parameters for the new program:

- For now, the plan is to affect the 120 students that the four teachers manage. In time, consideration will be given to extending the plan, or a modification of it, to other teams of interested teachers in the school.

- The plan will follow this time frame: From now (October) through the spring term and summer period, the new instructional program will be designed and developed; then a tryout with some students in the fall will be done. Full implementation by the following spring is planned.

- Initial funding will be available for the facilitator and to pay the four teachers for two weekend work periods per month during the school year, and for one month next summer. If the district is unable to provide additional funds for program development, money will be requested from other potential sources as needs are identified.

- Once development is completed, and the program is ready for full implementation, it should operate within an allocated school budget from the district.

Then Joan Stefans gives the team permission to start its planning. The principal relinquishes some control and decision making on the school level to the team members. She asks them to set a schedule and to keep her informed of their progress and any problems they may encounter. The team will periodically report to the total school faculty and district personnel on their plans and activities. Joan's last comment is to remind the team that together they are all accountable for the results of their decisions and actions to ensure that as many students as possible can be successful in the new program.

A VISION STATEMENT AND MISSION GOALS

With an awareness of the elements in the Stage 3 paradigm for education, the facilitator helps the team members start the planning process by expressing a vision for their instructional program. This is a statement of the beliefs and overall intent of the program; it provides a general direction for their planning.

One benefit for developing and agreeing on a vision statement is the opportunity it provides each teacher to describe his or her own position as to the nature of the potential program and what its emphasis should be. The facilitator stimulates the discussion, urging the teachers to be open-minded and creative in their thinking as ideas are generated and considered. As they proceed, he asks for clarifications—"*What does that mean?*" "*How do these factors relate?*" "*Is that really a Stage 3 thought?*"—and assists the group to reach a consensus statement. The give-

and-take of this discussion helps each teacher to clarify his or her beliefs and to become more aware of other positions as agreements are reached.

Here is their final vision statement:

> Every student at Stoneridge Middle School can learn, each to his or her highest potential level. It is the role of the school to guide each student, in terms of his or her learning style, to reach this level in a future-oriented educational program, by means of a variety of satisfying learning experiences.

At this point, the question to be answered is, *"What must happen in the school to accomplish this vision?"* The vision statement leads to a series of goals, which become the school's mission. They spell out the vision in more detail, like the goals developed by the team for Stoneridge (shown below).

These comprehensive goals state what the school is expected to accomplish as its mission. They become a commitment to action. Along with the vision statement, the mission goals become the framework within which the instructional program will be designed and developed.

INVOLVE PARENTS AND CAREGIVERS

Once the team feels comfortable with the vision statement and mission goals, they are shared with the principal and school district administrators. An orientation meeting is then set to involve parents in planning for the new program. After the anticipated benefits that students may derive are explained, parents can decide if they want their children to participate in the new program or to stay in a traditional

The school shall offer a strong support system for student learning so that the following goals can be accomplished for at least 90 percent of the students:

- Each student shall reach his or her individual potential in mastering basic knowledge and communication skills in reading, writing, speaking, and listening, or advance beyond that level.

- Each student shall acquire understanding and gain competencies in language arts, mathematics, the sciences, and the social studies, at least to the levels specified by the state educational accomplishments agenda, with evaluation based on individual growth rather than on group averages.

- Each student should be able to locate, process, and apply information in creative, realistic ways for critical thinking and problem solving.

- Each student shall recognize and respect the moral and democratic principles essential in American society.

- Each student shall become competent and comfortable in using technological resources for learning.

- Each student shall develop skills to be both a self-directed learner and a cooperative member of activity-oriented study groups.

- There shall be practical and realistic steps taken by the school to encourage and support parent participation with at least 60 percent of parents and caregivers involved.

- There shall be active involvement of community individuals and groups in the school's educational program.

class. A carefully planned presentation and follow-up discussion takes place. Parents are told that they will be kept informed as progress is made in planning and implementing the program. Their input, reactions, and comments are welcome, and they are encouraged to participate.

After the initial meeting with parents, the planning team, in consultation with the principal, decide to form a Parents/Community Advisory Committee. Through the efforts of this group, other parents and community members can be encouraged to become involved in the new program. Members of the committee will be invited to attend planning sessions, to offer suggestions for the developing new program, and to volunteer as teaching assistants, aides, or resource persons.

Agreed refinements are made in the vision statement and goals. Once they are finalized, each teacher willingly accepts them for implementation.

EXPECTED ACCOMPLISHMENT OF GOALS

A number of shortcomings faced by the school were identified on page 97. By gathering data relative to the present accomplishment of the stated goals, the planning team will have a baseline from which the new program can be developed. As they examine the situation, the teachers indicate criteria, as a percent of student success, that should be expected in the new program.

- Student achievement levels in basic subjects—95 percent of students reaching individual potential

- Students successfully completing academic and elective courses—90 percent

- Students completing an entire school year successfully—90 percent

- Students disciplined for behavior problems—5 percent or lower

- Student attitudes toward school, toward instructional methods for learning, and toward their fellow students, as observed and expressed on rating scales—90 percent positive

The team analyzes the data for present accomplishment levels for each goal. These levels can influence the design of the new program. Then after the program is fully implemented, evaluation results allow for comparison with the above desirable success levels. ◆

CHAPTER 16

Designing the Instructional Program

Three factors serve as the bases for designing the instructional program:

- The concepts specified for practices in Stage 3 of the McBeath model (Figure 1 on page 9).

- The stated goals of the new program (page 102).

- The results of pre-assessing students' present accomplishments and their attitudes toward school learning (page 103).

PROGRAM COMPONENTS AND INSTRUCTIONAL METHODS

In preparation for deciding on the methods of instruction, consultant Randy Lewis explains that all instruction can be organized within the following three major teaching/learning patterns. (For details of these patterns, see Chapter 9.)

- **Presentations** by a teacher or students to a class

- **Collaborative and interactive activities** within groups of students

- **Self-directed learning** and/or tutoring for individual students

With information and identified instructional needs, the team decides that it should provide the following broad kinds of learning experiences for students:

- Acquiring knowledge in **basic-skills subjects** to attain individual competencies on prerequisite, required, and advanced levels. This would take place through individual use of *self-directed learning* modules, tutorial instruction, and some group work.

- Acquiring knowledge and understandings in **academic areas** according to middle school curriculum framework requirement. The instruction will be integrated around *interdisciplinary thematic topics* through presentations by teachers, student group activities, and individual or team study.

- Experiencing higher-level intellectual processes and developing attitudes and social behaviors through student-chosen, **problem-based projects** that would be carried out by student groups working in school and in the community.

- Engaging in conventional knowledge and skill classes (visual and performing arts, introduction to foreign languages, physical education, health, survey of vocations, and so forth).

It is agreed that these four categories will comprise the education program for the 120 students under the direction of the four teachers. *What broad teaching and learning methods might be used to serve each instructional area?* See the illustration of program components and instructional methods on the following page.

Plan for Components of New Program at Stoneridge Middle School

COMPONENT	SUBJECT AREAS	INSTRUCTIONAL METHOD
Basic Skills	Reading Writing Speaking Listening	Self-directed learning and practice Tutorial supervision Student pairs
Academic Areas	Mathematics Literature Social Studies Sciences	Classroom experiences Establish interdisciplinary themes Presentations to classes with student interaction Student group activities
Student Projects	All subjects Realistic topics, problems, or issues	5–6 students in groups Select project Carry out operational plan Reports, presentations of results
Other Classes	Health Visual arts Physical education Electives	Conventional classes Regular instruction by other teachers

REVIEW LITERATURE ON INNOVATIVE PRACTICES

As their planning continues, team members agree that they need to know more about innovative practices in schools. While the teachers have access to some educational journals that report on new projects and programs, they want to examine resources that identify various features, personnel roles, success criteria, and so on.

Randy Lewis brings in some useful books treating various kinds of school reforms, model programs, and evidence of innovative successes. He also has given a special assignment to two graduate students. They are to conduct a survey of education literature, selecting articles that are pertinent to the goals of this project. Video recordings of new or successfully revised school program examples will be included. (See "References and Sources," Section H on page 167, and Section M on page 169.)

PROCEDURAL FEATURES OF THE NEW PROGRAM

As the teachers review reports, articles, and their own notes taken during earlier visits to nearby schools, certain practices become evident that have proven to be successful or that sound promising. At a Saturday meeting, they start to prepare a list of features within four categories that will be important when they start developing the details of their new program.

Administration

- Operate the project as a "school within the main school" and coordinate activities, use of facilities, and so on between the new program and the school's regular ongoing program.

- Use the "homeroom" concept as a base for students so each one has continual identity with a specific teacher; assign up to 30 students to one teacher for all years each student will be at Stoneridge.

- Use a flexible, non-graded approach to school organization.

- Combine subjects into an interdisciplinary or integrated thematic curriculum based on established curricular frameworks that direct knowledge, processes, and skills required within each curriculum area.

- Plan for daily flexible schedules and varying student activity times.

Students

- Guide students to assume increasing responsibility and accountability for their own learning and personal development.

- Provide variable time requirements for students to achieve agreed-upon objectives through various learning activities.

- Provide for participation of at-risk students in mixed ability groupings as feasible.

Instruction

- Design instructional activities so there are opportunities for large-group, small-group, and individual learning activities, with teachers becoming facilitators and consultants to individual students.

- Provide for instruction to extend beyond the school building.

- Accept results from state-approved standardized testing of students for comparison purposes, if measurements are based on comparable learning objectives treated in the new program.

- Design evaluation methods that are directly related to required outcomes, and report results in terms of the learning objectives they are designed to measure.

- Recognize student accomplishments in terms of each individual's potential and performance, rather than as compared to other students by conventional norm-referenced grading.

Support Personnel

- Encourage parent interest in the new program and encourage parents to participate in both instructional and non-instructional activities.

- Involve the library media specialist during planning for resource acquisition, facilities adaptation, and other instructional support.

- Use aides and students from the middle school, high school, and local university to guide, tutor, and coach students in various learning activities.

- Encourage persons from the community (government agencies, business, industry, health fields, recreation, and so forth) to participate when their skills and resources fit instructional needs.

- Use the Parents/Community Advisory Committee to encourage participation of the groups they represent, to offer suggestions, provide personnel and resources, and to serve as a sounding board for evaluating new practices.

- Develop a close relationship with personnel and resources from the nearby university, in part by obtaining help from both graduate students and those in the teacher education program.

As the planning continues, Randy makes contacts in the community for special equipment, service needs, and extra financial support. Preparation of grant proposals is considered.

PLANNING FOR CONVENTIONAL CLASSES

In addition to the three aspects of the program to be described, students will be assigned to (or will select from) regular classes in foreign languages, visual and performing arts, physical education, vocational subjects, and so forth. These classes are taught by other teachers in conventional ways, with coordination to the new program. For example, skills learned, as in art or shop classes, can be applied in project activities.

SCHEDULING THE NEW PROGRAM

Among the new parameters for this program is a time frame leading to implementation. The plan calls for design and development to take place from October through the following summer, tryout with any revisions during the next fall term, and full implementation in the spring.

As the components of the new program take shape, the matter of scheduling teachers and students is carefully considered. Since there is to be a variety of teaching and learning activities, with much responsibility given to the students, flexibility in scheduling is a necessity. This means moving away from the usual 45- to 50-minute periods in a uniform six-period school day.

With Randy's help, the teachers arrive at the following decisions and discuss them with the school principal:

1. Each teacher has a half-hour homeroom period each day with the same 25 to 30 students. During this time, announcements, schedules, and other administrative matters are handled. Students make progress reports on their projects. Other general interest matters receive attention.

2. The school day is divided into 90-minute blocks of time—two in the morning and two in the afternoon. During these periods, one or more related activities can take place as follows:

   • Self-directed learning in basic skills, tutorial assistance, testing, and so forth.

   • Interdisciplinary subject presentations by one or more teachers, followed by small-group discussions and activities.

   • Problem-based group project activities in school and in the community.

   • Regular classes offered in visual and performing arts, physical education, health, foreign languages, and so forth. Since these are conventional 45-minute classes, taught by other teachers in the school, students can take two of them during a 90-minute time block.

   • With modular scheduling, flexible arrangements from day to day can be made.

3. For the students in this program, the school day, instead of consisting of six hours of classes, would require seven hours of classes and activities—8:15 a.m. to 4:00 p.m., with 45 minutes for lunch and 5 minutes travel time between classes. (Note: Expanded schedules proposed here may require early and late bus transportation for students. Also, special consideration in terms of the teachers' union working arrangements contract needs attention.)

4. Each day, the teachers in the program would be free of assigned work with students for one 90-minute block. During this period, planning, consulting with colleagues, preparing materials, and scheduling special appointments can take place with individuals, groups of students, and parents. The illustration below shows a weekly schedule for one homeroom group of 25 to 30 students.

5. The teaching team plans to try out the new program components with 20 students during the following fall semester. Results will be evaluated and necessary revisions made.

6. As the program is implemented and ongoing, it may be advisable to seek a gradual extension of the school year from the usual 180 days to possibly 220 days.

The principal carefully reviews the proposed schedule and makes suggestions. When everyone has agreed on what is most reasonable and practical, the changes from conventional practices are presented to the superintendent and the school board. ◆

A One-Week Schedule for the New Program					
	M	**T**	**W**	**Th**	**F**
8:15	Homeroom . . . .
8:50	Acad	SDL	Other	Acad	Other
10:25	SDL	Acad	SDL	SDL	Acad
12:00	Lunch . . . .
12:50	Acad	Proj	Acad	Other	Proj
2:25	Other	Other	Proj	Other	Proj
4:00	End of Day—After-School Activities . . .

Key: Acad = Academic Subjects on Theme
SDL = Self-Directed Learning in Basic Skills
Proj = Student Group Project
Other = Other Conventional Classes

CHAPTER 17

Basic Subject Skills

There is evidence that students at Stoneridge vary in basic-skills competencies from the fourth-grade level to the tenth-grade level. The challenge is to help each individual attain at least his or her age-level requirements, and then to continue this growth during their remaining time at Stoneridge. Initially, this may require the use of review materials. Appropriate or advanced resources for continuous progress then will be needed. Some students will exhibit a readiness or motivation to attain competencies in basic skills beyond those recognized for their age levels. This would be encouraged and provided for, especially for gifted students.

TOPICS FOR SELF-STUDY

Randy Lewis helps the teachers to organize a list of topics on basic skills. The important question to answer is, *"What basic competencies should students have when they complete their education at Stoneridge?"* Subject curriculum frameworks and guides, units of study, and other available references are used.

In part, the list includes these topics with age-level competency performance requirements:

- **Reading**—vocabulary, word analysis, and comprehension

- **Writing**—prewriting plan, drafting, revising, and editing with attention to word usage, punctuation, grammar, capitalization, and spelling

- **Speaking**—organize ideas; express oneself in one-to-one communication, in small groups, and before a class

- **Listening**—receive, interpret, and respond to or use what is heard

- **Mathematics**—numbers, patterns and functions, logical reasoning, measurement, graphing, algebra, and geometry principles

The topics are organized into learning modules, and learning objectives are prepared for each one. (See pages 42–46.)

LOCATING RESOURCES

The primary instructional methods for attaining these basic-skills competencies would be student self-paced learning, supplemented with tutoring, paired, and group activities. Therefore, it becomes necessary to locate, evaluate, and select commercial self-study units or software, or to prepare new resources. Before starting the search, Randy works with the four teachers to establish criteria to objectively judge the suitability of materials. The team agrees with the nine instructional design features for self-paced learning materials in basic skills listed on page 49.

With help from the library media specialist, commercial materials are requested for preview. They are examined and evaluated in terms of subject learning objectives. Those selected are tested with students. Successful ones are chosen for student remedial, regular, and advanced study. It is also necessary to prepare additional modules to be certain that all basic-skills topics are satisfactorily treated. Under a teacher's direction, this is done by aides with the assistance of graduate students.

Managing self-directed learning

When a student satisfactorily completes study of a module or other self-study resource, the result is entered into a record-keeping software program, such as Guidebook or Grade Machine (produced by Educational Resources, Elgin, IL). This allows the teacher to follow the progress of each student. A printout can be used during teacher-parent conferences. Students can maintain records of their own, so each is directly aware of his or her progress. (See the example in Figure 8 on page 79.)

Necessary logistics

Once decisions are made about the self-study materials in basic skills, other questions need attention:

▶ *How many copies of each unit should be purchased or duplicated (with copyright permission)?*

Answer: This is to be a flexible program, so at any one time students will be involved in different activities. Arrangements might be made for up to 30 students to engage in self-instruction at once. Assuming that students will be working on various topics, this could require 10 copies of each module to be available.

▶ *What equipment and facilities are required for use?*

Answer: Following the reasoning in the answer above, 10 units of equipment for self-instructional use in basic skills are necessary. This can require such equipment as audiotape, CD, and video players. To support computer programs, assuming they will have the greatest use, at least five computers should be placed in each of the four teachers' regular classrooms. The school's centralized computer lab also can be used. The classroom computers will be interconnected as a network and attached to a file server that carries the courseware. A printer and other peripherals will be connected in each room. Also, 20 laptop computers with compatible software should be available for students to check out and use.

At this time, little physical change will be made in the four classrooms, although providing for network connections, upgrading electrical power as needed, and providing sufficient outlets for satisfactory use of the equipment will need to be arranged. Also, necessary tables or workstations will be requested, and the security of equipment will need to be considered.

▶ *What personnel are needed to supervise self-study activities, to assist students through tutoring, or to interact with small groups?*

Answer: While a teacher will be available for consultation to help students in deciding on learning objectives to pursue and in selecting resources to use, other aides or assistants, parents, and even older students can handle supervision and assistance responsibilities. At least two qualified persons should be in a room during self-study activities, and they should be fully oriented to the program materials and tutoring procedures. Peer assistance and tutoring by older students can also be advantageous.

▶ *What are funding needs at this stage?*

Answer: Printed and simple media materials may require an expenditure of $500 for each set of 10 copies of a module; 30 to 40 modules may be used, totaling up to $20,000. Costs for computer software vary widely, from about $50 per floppy disk or CD-ROM module to many thousands of dollars for a sophisticated learning system. For budgeting at this stage, $30,000 may be requested for software materials, and $6,000 for audiovisual equipment. The 20 computer stations and printers in the four classrooms will amount to about $25,000. The 20 laptop computers cost about $16,000. Installing network lines, additional electrical outlets, and minor renovations might be $1,000 per room, or $4,000 total. Thus, total cost is close to $100,000 to serve the 120 students.

At this stage of planning, the answers to these questions about logistics should be accepted as tentative. As further planning takes place, the needs may have to be clarified, treated in more detail, or reconsidered. ◆

CHAPTER 18

Interdisciplinary Subject Themes

The second component of this new program is teaching academic subjects. Since each teacher has competency in at least one of the four subject areas—language arts, social studies, sciences, or mathematics—there may be an initial urge to teach regular classes and assign work to students in each subject. Randy asks these questions:

▶ *In our everyday world, do not our experiences and out-of-school learning relating to a single idea or problem, cut across many subject areas?*

▶ *For any topic, what subject matter is needed, and what learning objectives should be accomplished?*

▶ *What guidelines can be obtained from the McBeath model of educational change (Figure 1 on page 9) to help with these selections?*

THE CONCEPT OF INTEGRATION

Randy cites these examples: a science worker, in addition to competency in a specialty, requires skills in careful reading, making measurements, and applying formulas or rules; a truck driver must interpret map directions, calculate fuel needs and costs, and be competent in operation of electronic equipment. Thus, knowledge and skills in any job require learning in many areas. Also, much literature we read has historical content significance. Therefore, Randy suggests, *"Shouldn't we integrate subjects in relevant, meaningful ways for students?"*

The teachers agree, but are still uncertain as to how they might implement an interdisciplinary method of teaching. They do recall that during a couple of the school visits, they saw cross-curricula classes being taught. That practice certainly made sense.

Randy follows with some research on interdisciplinary teaching. He locates reports and a couple of video examples of schools applying integrated-curricula methods that the group could examine and discuss. See "References and Sources," Section H, (page 167), including the Caine and Caine book that relates findings from brain-use studies (neuropsychology) to interdisciplinary educational methods. The evidence is that the brain searches for common patterns and connections among bits of information as they are received. Therefore, a real-life learning experience is not divided into discrete subjects, but actually contains within it elements relating to many disciplines. Frequently, this requires a multifaceted approach to thinking and doing.

After further discussion, it is agreed that integrating subjects with a thematic treatment wherever possible is the way to go. This means that by considering the relevant content areas for a theme, two or more teachers can plan and deliver classroom presentations and provide for related student activities.

One teacher reminds the group that the state curriculum frameworks for the four subject areas need to be reviewed. They specify the essential subject content for inclusion in teaching each discipline, and can provide the means to correlate content elements.

To better understand how this concept of integrating subject areas might be developed, the team decides to engage in brainstorming on a theme. The theme of early exploration is chosen, and this question is asked: *"What might be included from each subject discipline relating to this theme?"* (See the example below for the teachers' plan.)

Content and Activities for the Interdisciplinary Theme of Early Exploration

Social Studies—Reading and viewing media on European history and geography of the Age of Exploration

Mathematics—Designing and interpreting maps and charts showing the explorations described

Science—Considering the scientific discoveries, transportation, and communication methods that made the explorations possible

English—Reading and analyzing novels, poems, diaries, and other literature describing experiences and ways of life during the Age of Exploration

---

With this practical example, it is better understood by the teachers how such a procedure can be used—first, to select an overall theme in a curriculum area, such as social studies in the above example; and second, to find logical topics in other disciplines that relate. It may not always be easy to do this for all four subject areas. Sometimes only math and science can be related, or English and social studies. These combinations are called *multidisciplinary.* And let us not forget, one teacher points out, that curricula areas such as art, music, industrial studies, home economics, and even physical education may help to engage students in applying knowledge gained from academic subjects to the theme.

There may be some themes in which necessary content in one discipline cannot be easily related to other disciplines for middle-school students. In such instances, individual teachers can design and prepare single-subject presentations with follow-up activities for students.

Randy then explains that in planning interdisciplinary units, three instructional matters require careful attention:

- Include the use of various media to make class presentations both motivational and informative, while providing for student involvement and homework assignments.

- Form groups of six to eight students for activities that include further study discussions, reporting, and applications of the theme across the treated subject areas.

- During the above, help students see connections among the subject disciplines within the theme.

PLANNING PROCEDURE

Each interdisciplinary teaching team follows this instructional planning procedure:

1. Share and examine each teacher's curriculum framework, curriculum guides, textbooks, supplemental materials, and media resources.

2. Choose and agree on a number of themes that logically require interdisciplinary treatment.

3. Assign one teacher as a "theme leader" to coordinate planning and development.

4. Indicate content in each subject area that will become integrated with the theme.

5. Develop objectives that will lead to learning outcomes.

6. Review background preparation that students need and decide how to pretest for it. Indicate remedial study that may be necessary.

7. Decide on the teaching/learning activities for the theme within the following areas:

- Teacher presentations about 30 to 45 minutes in length, including media materials (lecture segments not to run longer than about 10 minutes without some planned or voluntary student participation)

- Follow up with homework assignments and small-group activities

8. Decide on materials for use during presentations or in group activities. Locate or prepare materials.

9. Develop detailed lesson plans.

10. Plan assessment of learning in terms of the stated learning objectives.

11. Decide the orientation necessary for assistants who will handle small-group follow-up activities.

Under the direction of the school library media specialist, university students or aides are assigned to help teachers research their subjects and to locate or prepare materials for their presentations. Some categories of resources considered for student follow-up uses include: video recordings, CD-ROMs, and computer software for information, simulations, and other interactive experiences. Also, consideration is given to finding knowledgeable persons who might be invited into a class, locally, or contacted through televised distance learning reception, e-mail, or by searching Web sites on the Internet.

As the planning takes shape for the initial themes, the group decides on the following questions as the criteria for judging the success of their planning efforts:

- Does each teacher feel comfortable with the theme and its treatment of subject content?

- Will the theme be of interest to students?

- Is each teacher working on a theme able to contribute meaningful content and activities?

- Do the learning objectives being written require higher levels of student learning?

- Do we have appropriate materials available to support activities, or do new materials need to be developed or obtained?

- Are the follow-up small-group activities meaningful and worthwhile experiences for students?

- Do evaluation methods of learning correlate directly with the objectives, going beyond measuring recall of information by requiring application, analysis, and synthesis of the information?

One teacher asks, "In terms of Stage 3 practices, should we involve students in selecting themes for study?" The group agrees that later on, after both teachers and students have experience with a few themes and feel comfortable with this new procedure, groups of students may be asked to participate in choosing and planning themes.

See the example (Figure 11 on page 114) for full development of an interdisciplinary theme. ◆

FIGURE 11
Sample Interdisciplinary Theme: The Industrial Revolution

I. Goal
To understand the 18th Century in England, during which major changes began in all aspects of society

II. Subject Content
  A. Setting the Stage
    England in the early 18th Century
  B. Developments in Industry
    Textiles
    Coal use in blast furnaces and forges for making iron and steel
    Pottery manufacturing
  C. Developments of Power
    Water wheel
    Steam engine
  D. Developments in Transportation
    Roads and canals
    Iron bridges
    Steam locomotive and railroads
    Steamboats
  E. Effects on British Society
    Daily life
    Home to factory work
    Industrial cities
    Owners' relationships to workers
  F. General Impact
    Crystal Palace Great Exhibit 1851
    Environmental problems
    Prosperity and decline

III. Subject Area Learning Objectives
  A. Social Studies
    Describe the conditions of life in England in the early 18th Century
    Examine the developments in industry, power, and transportation during the 18th Century
    Analyze the effects on society during industrial developments
    Assess future changes that would result from these industrial and other developments
    Compare 18th-Century developments with effects of "Computer Revolution" in the Information Age
  B. Science
    Describe how various inventions were created and operated
    Assemble or construct and apply inventions for doing practical work
    Identify five fundamental scientific principles applied in inventions
  C. Mathematics
    Illustrate the output of various products during the 18th and 19th Centuries in graphic form

Convert British currency of the time to U.S. equivalents
Compare cost of living and wages during the Industrial Revolution with costs and wages today
  D. English
    Discuss conditions and developments of the time as described in literature of contemporary writers
    Report on biographies of leaders and inventors during the Industrial Revolution
    Describe how developments during the 18th Century influenced times that have followed

IV. Teaching and Learning Activities
  A. Teacher Presentation
    Treat objectives in four subjects using pictures, slides, and video to supplement verbal information and explanations
  B. Student Activities during Presentations
    Complete outlines
    Take notes
    Engage in discussions
  C. Student Work in Small Groups (and Homework)
    Literature readings (novels, biographies, nonfiction) in addition to CD-ROMs and videos
    Reports (written and oral) on readings and topics (e.g., "Create a script or TV news program describing an event during the Industrial Revolution and interviewing participants," or "Write a newspaper article, with photos or art, on an invention during the Industrial Revolution")
    Respond to the following: "Contrast your daily life today with what it would have been like if you had lived during the Industrial Revolution"
    Constructing inventions
    Math projects
    Displays and presentations to class
    Resources: library materials—texts, references, novels, nonfiction, biographies, plays, CD-ROMs, historical videodiscs and videotapes, word-processing and page-design software

V. Evaluation of Learning
  A. Tests on historical and other subject area content from presentations, readings, reports, etc.
  B. Rating of group and individual work
    Reports on readings
    Descriptions of inventions
    Other writing assignments
    Design and operation of inventions
    Preparation of graphs and other math items
    Display or group presentation

CHAPTER 19

Problem-Based Projects

The third part of this new program involves student problem-solving projects. In exploring how to handle this component, the team considers these questions:

▶ *How can we go beyond the limited small-group activities that are part of the integrated curriculum study component of the program?*

▶ *How would students profit from experiences that require them to explore and analyze real problems, perform research, share information, plan actions, or synthesize components to create new products or reach solutions for problems, and then report results?*

These are the kinds of questions that the members of the teaching team now face as they search for a way to extend student learning in keeping with the mission goals. Team members believe that successful reflection, higher-order thinking, and problem solving through work on meaningful projects can be the answer. They agree that groups of cooperating students should be formed. Each group would then select a suitable topic of interest or concern and go to work.

With these initial ideas, Randy helps the teachers formulate a plan. It requires attention to the following features:

1. Organize students into groups.

2. Explain purpose for this project.

3. Specify roles for adult coordinators (see "Resources for Use" on page 117).

4. Suggest topics or problems for student choice, or consider a student-selected topic according to acceptance criteria.

5. Guide groups in assigning responsibilities.

6. Indicate resources available.

7. Monitor student decisions for operational procedures to carry out the project.

8. Explain format for results.

9. Set a schedule for completion.

10. Establish criteria or requirements for success.

11. Evaluate student presentation and report.

COMPOSITION OF STUDENT GROUPS

Five to six students will comprise a group. Students should have the freedom to form their own groups, although a teacher can "suggest" modifications in order to have a balanced group. This means there should be both *leaders* and *followers*, *researchers* and *doers*, and other combinations of personalities, qualifications, and interests within a heterogeneous group. It is understood that each student must participate actively in one way or another to make a group successful. When further projects are implemented later in the school year, different student groups can be formed.

Each student group selects a group leader, whose responsibilities are to:

- call meetings of the group

- help the group agree on a plan to follow

- delegate duties and responsibilities, as agreed to or accepted by each member

- help to set a schedule for activities

- make contact with resource persons through the adult coordinator

- advise the coordinator of any problems encountered as the group proceeds with its work

- report progress to the coordinator and to the teacher

- coordinate preparation of the final report and presentation of group results

PURPOSE OF THE PROJECT

Students are to be clearly informed of the purposes for the project in which they will engage. They are to select and investigate a topic, problem, or issue that is of interest to them, and acquire an in-depth understanding of it. Then, after research and careful thought, they will devise a reasonable answer, solution, or product. The students' final responsibility will be to prepare a written report and present the results to their fellow students and guests.

SUGGESTED TOPICS FOR STUDENT SELECTION

The four teachers make available a list of issues that are suitable projects for middle school students. Each student group selects a topic that interests its members. Preferably, a specific subject becomes the activity for only one group. A group might come up with a variation of the topic, or its own topic to investigate. If this happens, the topic will be discussed with a teacher who examines the group's goal and plan to make certain the topic is suitable and can be handled in the allotted time.

The box at the top of the next column contains a number of suggested project questions that are ideally suited for investigation by middle school students.

- Is there a future for electric automobiles?

- Where does our garbage go? Can recycling work?

- How can we judge the values offered by commercial entertainment (TV, movies, computer games, etc.)?

- What do middle school students eat for lunch? Is it nutritious?

- What are alternative forms of energy to oil and gas? How efficient are they?

- In what ways can genetically engineered foods or new organisms for medical treatments be beneficial or potentially harmful?

- What are other ways to permit public voting in statewide and national elections than by casting ballots in person (with advantages and disadvantages)?

PROCEDURE TO CARRY OUT A PROJECT

The project activity provides more sophisticated learning opportunities than does conventional instruction: Students must take the initiative, accept responsibilities, make choices, reach consensus, and engage in conceptual thinking and other higher-level intellectual skills.

Teachers and coordinators provide guidance, ask questions to help clarify understanding, and otherwise offer coaching assistance. When the project assignment is introduced to the students, an example of a potential project might be presented, with the procedures to accomplish it being explained and illustrated.

Student responsibilities in the project include the following:

1. Defining project objectives to be investigated and outcomes to be accomplished.

2. Establishing a timeline for procedures and individual responsibilities within the group.

3. Setting a daily or weekly schedule for activities.

4. Locating and acquiring information about the subject or problem, including library print and media resources, information databases, interviews with selected individuals, visits to locations of interest or observation of activities in the community, and communication with other knowledgeable persons through regular mail, e-mail, and on the World Wide Web.

5. Analyzing and organizing the information collected.

6. Deciding when the group is prepared to reach closure.

7. Reaching agreement within the group for conclusions and generating recommendations, or identifying the need for further work.

8. Preparing to present the results, findings, and/or recommendations.

RESOURCES FOR USE

Two different kinds of personnel services are available to the student groups. One consists of persons who *supervise, guide,* and *coach* each group. Because of the number of groups required to organize the 120 students, individual teachers need to make contact with many groups during the working periods. Each group would have assigned to it one or more coordinators—an aide, parent, other volunteer, or older student—with direct responsibilities to the group.

The second personnel service is the *resource* category. This covers everyone from the school library media specialist, other teachers with special experiences, aides, parents, qualified senior citizens, older students with special knowledge or talents (such as guiding a student group to prepare a video recording), community business or service individuals, legislators, and university specialists. Any person might be called upon for direct information, technical assistance, advice, opinions, or to serve other purposes in terms of the project needs.

It is difficult to indicate specific resources for use, since each project will have its own needs. In general, anything or anyone available in the school (including art, music, or vocational teachers) and in the community might be useful. The "coaching" teacher or

assistant of a group helps students to make a reasonable selection of resources for use.

For practical experience, the use of technological resources such as videos, CD-ROMs, computer databases, the Internet or other computer network services, and word-processing programs for letter writing and report preparation should be encouraged. Video production equipment and presentation software are available for student use in documenting and reporting project activities and results.

FORMAT FOR RESULTS

One or more products will be required to show accomplishments of stated objectives. Suggested forms may include the following:

- a daily journal as a diary prepared by each student

- a written report; a story or script for a play, video, or slide program; or other product to illustrate project results

- a performance or presentation made on a stage before other students, teachers, and parents

- a media production, a computer program, an exhibit of a constructed product, or an art display

- prepared materials collected as individual student portfolios

SCHEDULE FOR COMPLETION

This matter receives careful consideration by the teaching team. Obviously, a project for middle school students cannot be as demanding as one required for high school or college-level students. But it should require enough activity time that students become seriously immersed in the work—possibly two hours a day, three days per week, for three to five weeks.

CRITERIA FOR SUCCESS

As project activities proceed, the adult working with each group makes certain that the students know they will be responsible for some form of final product, as described above. The evaluation criteria—in the form of a checklist or rating scale—are prepared by the teachers and made available to the students. In this way, the students will know the factors by which the quality of their results will be judged—by themselves and by other students, teachers, and assistants. A sample evaluation instrument is shown below. ◆

Sample Checklist and Rating Scale for Evaluating Student Group Activities

Checklist: Were the following features satisfactorily included in the group's project presentation? Circle YES or NO for each item.

1. Indicating objectives for project   YES NO

2. Explaining value or importance of topic   YES NO

3. Describing procedure for gathering information   YES NO

4. Explaining problems or unusual situations encountered and how overcome   YES NO

5. Using media (type_____) to support the verbal presentation   YES NO

6. Involving the audience   YES NO

7. Stating conclusions and recommendations, or showing results in form of _____   YES NO

8. Replying to audience questions or observations   YES NO

9. Participation by each group member   YES NO

Rating Scale: How do you rate the inclusion or quality of each feature in the group's presentation? Place a check mark on each line.

1. Indicating objectives for project

LOW   MEDIUM   HIGH

2. Explaining value or importance of project

LOW   MEDIUM   HIGH

3. Describing procedure for gathering information

LOW   MEDIUM   HIGH

And so on . . .

CHAPTER 20

Evaluating the Program

Program evaluation starts with a review of the stated mission goals (see page 102). The key is *success in learning for as many students as possible.* On the basis of this requirement, two types of program evaluation become necessary: (1) **formative evaluation** (see pages 79–80) and (2) **summative evaluation** (see Chapter 13).

FORMATIVE EVALUATION

When the program components are being tried out with some students or implemented with a class for the first time, careful judgments of its success are made. Answers to the questions on pages 79–80 help the teachers decide what revisions in content, objectives, activities, resources chosen and used, personnel services, schedules, facilities use, and so forth may be necessary to improve the program. Necessary changes are made; then with the next use, the program is evaluated again for effectiveness.

SUMMATIVE EVALUATION

Randy Lewis explains to the teachers that their summative evaluation starts by re-examining the shortcomings initially identified. For Stoneridge Middle School, some of these needs are stated on page 97 and then restated with anticipated criteria for success on page 103. The question examined now is, *"How well does the instructional program overcome those shortcomings, meet the anticipated criteria, and serve the school's mission goals?"*

If any of the following measures do not reach an accepted standard, then program revisions are considered. This evaluation is repeated at the end of each school year.

Learning effectiveness

Effectiveness answers the question, "To what degree do students accomplish the learning objectives prescribed for each unit or component of the program?" The results are tabulated with conclusions like these:

> - Ninety-six percent of the students accomplished at least 90 percent of the objectives in basic skills.
>
> - Eighty-six percent of the students satisfied 80 percent of the objectives for the three interdisciplinary thematic units.
>
> - Student project results indicate *very good* or *good* ratings for 23 of 26 group projects.

Comparisons can also be made between pretest and post-test results in academic subjects. (See example in Figure 10 on page 85.)

Cost benefits

As shown in the "Program Cost per Student" illustration on page 120, cost benefits (also termed *cost effectiveness*) are determined by measuring the sum of all operational expense categories required (personnel, materials and supplies, equipment and media resources, overhead costs), divided by the number of students taught (120 in this program).

Program Cost per Student	
INSTRUCTIONAL COSTS	
Teachers (4 @$40,000 each)	$160,000
Aides	60,000
Updating equipment and media	20,000
Materials and supplies	30,000
Overhead (administration, utilities, maintenance, transportation, insurance, etc.)	100,000
Total for 120 students	**$370,000**
Instructional cost per student	**$3,083**

The results of this analysis can be accepted as beneficial or as requiring revisions if considered to be too expensive for the resulting learning. The cost per student may be compared with similar programs either in the school or elsewhere, and a rating assigned in comparison.

Attitudes and Reactions

Attitudes and reactions are determined either by observations or questionnaires. (A set of sample questions for the Stoneridge Middle School program is shown below.)

After the results of the evaluations are tabulated, conclusions are drawn as to the acceptability of outcomes. Necessary modifications in the program are made for when it is next taught. ◆

Questions for Groups to Evaluate the New Program

For Teachers
1. How well did the new program serve the educational needs of your students?
2. How useful did you find to be the assistance you received from the facilitator, Dr. Randy Lewis?
3. Which components of the program were most successful?
4. Which were weak and will need more work?
5. How did you react to working with a team on curriculum planning and interdisciplinary teaching?

For Staff and Volunteers
1. How successful was the new program?
2. Was your role in the program important? If so, for what reasons?
3. How do you believe students have reacted to the program?

For Parents
1. Do you understand the purpose for and organization of the new program in which your son or daughter participated?
2. Do you feel the program has been successful? Any suggestions for improvement?
3. What one part of the program has been most useful to your child?
4. If you filled a participating role, did you enjoy it? In what way do you believe your work was of value to the program?

For Students
1. How well do you feel this new program provided you with an education?
2. What part or parts of the program did you find the most useful for your learning?
3. What suggestions do you have for improving the program?

CHAPTER 21

Planning to Continue and Extend the New Program

By the time the new program has been in full operation for one year, the four teachers have guided their students toward competencies in basic skills, developed and taught five interdisciplinary themes, and their students have completed three small-group problem-based projects. With these experiences, the teachers become more confident and capable in managing and handling all aspects of their new program. The need for services of the facilitator, Randy Lewis, is then reduced.

REPORTING PLANS AND PROGRESS

As components of the new program move through the planning cycle—design, development, and try-out—progress reports are made to the school principal. Difficult questions and problems relating to support services (facilities, materials equipment, personnel, funding, schedules, and so forth) are considered with the principal. Recommendations and advice from the facilitator are helpful in making decisions and taking action.

A critical factor for the acceptance and success of any new endeavor is to keep a variety of interested persons well informed. This serves to provide information and advise them of developments, motivate interest, encourage participation, and request feedback and suggestions. In this situation, providing for ongoing communication is most important while the school change process is becoming established.

There are at least seven groups with whom this interaction is necessary.

- Other teachers in the school
- Local and state school administrators
- Parents of students
- Involved community representatives and civic organizations
- Sponsoring agencies that support the program financially or with services
- College of education faculty and administrators at the nearby university
- Publicity organizations, including local newspapers and radio/television stations

As indicated in various places throughout this book, this communication can take place through:

- meetings to inform and discuss goals and developments
- displays and reports of student work
- student activities and projects documented on videotape
- written reports, newsletters, and publicity releases describing the program and its components as development takes place and when the program is implemented

- presentations at educational conferences and articles written for journals, and a school-based Web page on the Internet

EXTENSION WITHIN THE SCHOOL

As design, development, and tryout phases of the program progress, other teachers in the school become involved as follows.

- They receive progress reports made to the school faculty.

- They sit in on planning sessions, and they are encouraged to offer reactions and suggestions.

- They observe instructional sessions and student learning activities, and talk with students to obtain their impressions and reactions.

- They work with students who require instruction and assistance in projects involving health, art, music, home economics, shop skills, and so forth.

Over time, many of the teachers at Stoneridge indicate their willingness to become active in the new program. Periodically, the principal forms new interdisciplinary teams. Thus, there is a gradual transition toward a total school effort to complete transformation.

While the facilitator orients new teaching teams, it is decided that at least one of the original team teachers now has the experience to handle developmental work with them. Thus the systematic change process, as initiated, is continuing with the additional teacher teams. Also, new aides and graduate students become involved in the program. (With the interest created in systematic instructional planning, some teachers pursue graduate degrees in instructional technology at the university.)

The new teams profit from the experiences of those already in the program. The vision statement and mission goals (see page 102) are discussed and accepted with some modifications. The self-directed learning component in basic skills requires the same resources (additional copies are prepared or purchased). Funds are obtained to add computers to each teacher's classroom. Academic subject planning, then thematic selections, and student problem-based team projects, while modified according to specific student needs, interests, and teacher preferences, follow the same general practices as originally planned.

Gradually, most teachers buy into the accepted changes in the school's educational program, adding their own interpretations and interests. While the few teachers who do not want to participate could continue to teach conventional classes (and some parents might prefer these methods for their children), they are encouraged to transfer to other schools.

Parent meetings, including the participation of those whose children are now in the new program, continue to be held. Responses are encouraged. Community and business representatives frequently are invited to the school. Since additional students need to carry out some of their project work in the community, ongoing contacts are extended. Membership in the Parents/Community Advisory Committee is broadened, and the activities of members are increased.

In addition to the innovative instructional program, extracurricular activities receive attention. Student government, athletic programs, after-school activities, cultural events, and other enrichment functions are important in serving the school's mission goals. They are not neglected in this new program.

EFFECTS ON THE SCHOOL DISTRICT

Periodically throughout the planning and development process, the district superintendent, the school board, and other school principals are informed of progress and problems encountered at Stoneridge. As the program becomes operational, they visit the school periodically, observe and talk with the teachers involved, and hear from students and parents. Many administrators and board members also attend orientation and reporting sessions for parents. Reports continue to be made to the administration, including presentations by students of their activities and project results.

State Department of Education personnel and legislators are invited to observe and become familiar with the new program at Stoneridge Middle School. There are standards, state regulations, and legal matters, as well as policies and procedures that need to be examined for revision or even elimination in order to support, rather than hinder, the development and extension of such a new program.

For both educational merits and public relations purposes, teachers in the program are encouraged to report about the new program, their experiences, and those of students (including student "show-and-tell" sessions). These presentations take place at district, state, and national conference meetings. The teachers can write articles for journals and cooperate with the news media through interviews about the new program.

An important aspect of such a systematically designed middle school program is how well it correlates with both the feed-in elementary schools and the feed-to high school. The Stoneridge teachers become aware of the preparation and experiences students receive prior to attending the middle school and any remediation necessary. On the other side, the high school learns details of the new program and how well students are prepared for the ninth grade. Therefore, there can be pressures on the elementary schools to improve, and the high school can fit these middle school students more confidently into its program.

As the school program moves from "new" to "ongoing," it is decided that other teachers in the district middle schools that are starting to consider changes in their own programs should visit Stoneridge. Then, in addition to just getting a feel for the program, teachers volunteer to become members of an interdisciplinary team at Stoneridge for six months or a year to directly experience the new instructional procedures.

Thus, Stoneridge serves as a practical hands-on demonstration school site. Teachers return to their schools with experience that can be the starting point for their own school restructuring efforts. These teachers recognize the value of the facilitator-led planning team, the systematic instructional design process, the Parents/Community Advisory Committee, and the use of community support personnel. Based on their identified needs, the instructional plans that will be designed in the other schools may differ appreciably from the pattern at Stoneridge and still improve the quality of learning in that school.

In time, the total nature of education within this unified district, from elementary grades through high school, can be significantly changed and improved.

As other administrators and teachers visit at Stoneridge, a computer network is established among educators interested in sharing their ideas, experiences, instructional units, resources, and questions. This process offers needed collegial support for those involved in improving the education of their students.

Other schools in the district become interested in systematically restructuring their programs, and funds are set aside within the district to support development. Consideration is given to redirecting 2 to 5 percent of the total district's budget for capital outlay to finance systematic school program innovations.

EFFECTS AT THE UNIVERSITY

When graduate students from the university participate in the new program design, development, and implementation processes, they have many worthwhile experiences that can serve them well in their own professional careers. There are also implications for teacher education within the college of education. As previously indicated, teacher education interns and student teachers first observe and later work with the teachers in the new program. They serve as tutors and assist student groups both with academic activities and with their group projects. Such experiences can better prepare these future teachers for systemic changes and new Stage 3 teaching roles in keeping with the McBeath transformational model introduced on page 9. Also, training of instructional designers for service in schools is expanded.

After discussing the merits of the new program with the facilitator, Randy Lewis, and teacher education students, the dean of the education college and many education professors visit the new program. They talk with the principal, the teaching team, and participating students. The result is that changes are gradually made in the teacher education curriculum and course activities. These can widely affect the educational community as graduates obtain teaching and administrative positions in the area. ◆

APPENDIX B

Students Make It Happen!

A description of how students in the middle school described in Appendix A participate in the newly designed instructional program

CHAPTER 22

Introducing Two Students

Our story starts with the introduction of two seventh-grade students, whom we follow as they become engaged in the new school program.

NANCY MARTIN

Nancy usually awakens just before 7 a.m. Time to get ready for another school day. She washes, thoughtfully selects a sweatshirt and jeans, then dresses and heads downstairs for breakfast.

The previous evening, Nancy helped her mother set up for breakfast—juice in the refrigerator, cold cereal or soaked grain for cooking, bread ready for toasting, and low-fat milk with protein powder. Nancy's father is already at the table looking through the morning newspaper. She kisses him good morning and prepares to eat.

"Hi guys." With these words a few minutes later, Howard, Nancy's older brother, comes in. He's a bit sleepy-eyed, carrying a book and some papers.

"What are you working on?" asks his dad.

"I have to discuss a British writer; describe his personality, literary accomplishments, and attitudes toward Great Britain during the Victorian age."

"Who are you doing it on?" queries Nancy.

"I was given William Butler Yeats. He doesn't sound too interesting, from what I've read. It's kind of a stupid assignment, but you know some of the things Mrs. Greene likes to do in class. We'll have a tea with her acting as Queen Victoria. Each of us has to answer questions about our writer."

"Sounds interesting to me. It's all part of your education," states his dad. "Remember, good grades are important if you want to get into a quality engineering school."

"Yeah, I know," nods Howard.

Then Nancy says, "I hope I don't have to do stuff like that when I get to high school. There certainly are more important things to learn. Sounds like a waste of time."

"OK, kids. You might not see the purpose for something you are learning, but I'm sure it'll be important for you in time," counsels their father.

As the exchange ends, Nancy's mother enters the kitchen. She hugs the children and checks what they are eating. Shortly thereafter, the father glances at the clock and announces he's got to get to the office. He gives goodbye kisses to Nancy and his wife and a handshake to Howard.

As he leaves the room, Howard calls out, "Hey, Dad! Can I use the computer to quickly type out this material?"

"Sure, go ahead," is the reply, "but don't be late for school."

Then Nancy's mother reminds her about her piano lesson after school today. Nancy makes a face, but nods when her mother states that she'll pick her up from school at 3:30 p.m. Nancy excuses herself to brush her teeth, get her schoolbooks, and walk to the school bus stop.

BOBBY HESTER

Bobby Hester's mother bangs on the bedroom door, calling out, "You boys better get up and get ready for school!"

Mumbles are heard through the door, but little immediate activity. She turns to a young daughter, Mary Lou, who is starting to dress beside the sofa on which she sleeps.

"Tell your sister that you girls gotta meet me at that charity place after school to get some clothes. You both are growing so fast."

"OK, Mom," replies Mary Lou. "I'll tell Jean. I'm hungry for breakfast."

"There's still some bread and jam, but just a little milk. Better share it with your sister. I don't know what the boys will eat. And if they don't get moving, they'll miss their buses. Anyway, I gotta go pick up food stamps when that office opens."

Bobby comes out of the bedroom, followed by his older brother, Mark, who goes to high school. They are both still sleepy are are struggling into their clothes.

"I've gotta meet some of my buddies over at Tom's place," says Bobby.

"You'd better go to school and learn somethin' today."

"Heck, it ain't important to me," scowls Bobby. "I learn more from the guys than from those teachers . . . except for Mr. Schmidt in science. His stuff's good, but I don't understand a lot if it."

His mother says, "It's up to you. You better learn, so you can get a job like your older brother has after school."

"Yeah, working in that fast-food shop. I'll do better than that with the guys," responds Bobby.

His mother looks annoyed as Bobby leaves the apartment. When he gets to the street, he pauses for a moment, then shakes his head in disgust, and turns to the school bus stop where other kids are standing. "Might as well go to school today," he thinks. He had taken off early yesterday, and he knows he'll be in real trouble if he skips school today.

Bobby finds a piece of a candy bar in a pocket. This will be breakfast, unless he can bum something more from one of the younger kids at school.

When the bus arrives at Stoneridge Middle School, Nancy, Bobby, and the other students mix with those already on the playground. Nancy joins a group of girls who talk about TV shows they saw last night and joke about some of the boys they see standing nearby.

Bobby finds a couple of sixth graders he knows. They're talking about sports, then just as Bobby joins them, the school bell rings, and everyone moves into the building to their homerooms. So starts their school day. ◆

CHAPTER 23

Introducing the New Program

The Martin family finishes dinner. Nancy's father is doing the dishes, while Nancy and her brother begin their homework assignments. Mr. Martin then settles down to finish reading the newspaper he started at breakfast. After a few minutes, he remarks, "Have you seen this article about the school board considering a new educational program at Nancy's school?"

"No, what's that about?" asks Nancy.

"I've heard there's something going on," replies Mrs. Martin. "Betty Moore told me she is in a planning group looking at other school programs to find ideas for improving the one at Stoneridge."

"It says that Mrs. Stefans, the principal, presented an analysis of the present school program to the board with suggestions for revising it," explains Mr. Martin. "Five parents and four teachers accompanied her. They will become the planning team to examine and start revising the school program. A professor from the university will help them. The board approved some money to support their work. I wonder what they're going to do that is new . . . oh, here it says . . . 'Parents and guardians of students who will be in the eighth grade next fall will receive a letter about the new program. They will give permission if they want their child in the program.'"

"Sounds interesting . . . We'll wait and see if you're involved, Nancy. I've felt some parts of their teaching should be improved."

There is no early information about the new program available from the newspaper or other source at Bobby Hester's home.

A few days later, during a homeroom period, Mr. Stulforth informs the students about the proposed new program they may have in the eighth grade next year. He tells them that their new homeroom teacher, Ms. Lopez, along with Mr. Brown, Mr. Larson, and Mrs. Starr, are working on the plan for the program.

Students ask questions:

"What's going to be new?"

"Will we still be in regular classes . . . with our friends?"

"Will it help us in high school?"

"Will we have to be in the new program if we don't like it?"

Mr. Stulforth explains that he is unable to answer their questions right now. He then distributes sealed envelopes from Mrs. Stefans and emphasizes the importance of the enclosed letter. He instructs the students to take the letters home for their parents or guardians to read.

Nancy recalls the article in the newspaper her father had read. "This must be about the new program," she thinks.

When she gives the letter to her mother that afternoon, the two of them sit down as her mother reads:

Dear Parent or Guardian,

There have been concerns expressed about the quality of education your children receive at Stoneridge Middle School. I've heard this from parents as well as from our teachers.

We have done some analysis of student learning levels and students' attitudes toward school. The results are disappointing. I met with a few parents, and they feel their children should be doing better.

With the approval of the school superintendent and the school board, we are examining ideas for improving the education of our students. Four teachers, with the help of some parents, are exploring an entirely new approach to teaching their subjects.

We are inviting all parents who will have children in the eighth grade next year to meet with us. We would like your thoughts about the present school program and how you feel it is serving your children. Also, we will tell you about the new ideas being explored. On April 14 at 7 p.m., the meeting will take place in the school auditorium. Dr. Fiorino, the superintendent, will be there. After the meeting, a parents' advisory committee will be formed to assist us.

Following the meeting, each family will be asked to decide if their child might participate in the new program. Four classes, totaling 120 students, will start the new program next fall. We may have to conduct a lottery selection if too many request inclusion of their children. The permission slip will be mailed to all parents following the meeting. Please watch for it, mark it, and return it promptly.

All of us at Stoneridge are looking forward to this examination of our program and the potential for new and exciting changes at the school. We are counting on your involvement. Please meet with us on the 14th.

Sincerely,

Joan Stefans, Principal

"Sounds interesting, but no details here," says Mrs. Martin.

"Yes, I'd like to know more about what they're going to do," adds Nancy.

"Show the letter to your dad this evening," directs Mrs. Martin, "and I'll tell him to hold the 14th open for that meeting. We both should attend."

On his way home, Bobby wonders what's in the letter he was given at school. He doesn't think his mother will be very interested in any changes in the school program. When he gets home, his mother isn't there.

That evening, after dinner, the TV set is turned on while Mark, Bobby's older brother, helps Mrs.

Hester wash the dishes. Bobby, without much enthusiasm, starts his homework at the dinner table. As he opens a textbook, he remembers the letter that he had slipped inside the front cover.

"Hey, Mom, here's a letter I'm supposed to give you."

"What's it about? Are you in trouble?" asks Mrs. Hester, taking the letter. "I sure don't need any more problems with you."

"Naw. It's about a new program they're gonna have," retorts Bobby.

"That's their business. Why are they telling me?" queries Mrs. Hester.

"I dunno," Bobby remarks as he turns back to his work.

His mother opens the envelope and glances through the letter. "There's a meeting in a few weeks about a new school program, and I gotta decide whether you should be in it," she explains.

"Are you gonna go?" asks Bobby.

His mother mumbles an incoherent answer as she turns to dry the dishes.

Three days before April 14, reminder postcards about the forthcoming meeting arrive at the two homes. The Martins plan to attend. Mrs. Hester thinks she'll go, as long as Bobby or his brother will be home to watch over their young sisters.

SELECTING STUDENTS FOR THE NEW PROGRAM

A few days after the meeting, a new letter is mailed to all parents of next year's eighth-grade students, whether or not they had attended the meeting:

Dear Parent or Guardian,

At the meeting on April 14, we informed all parents attending about plans to initiate a new instructional program for eighth-grade students at Stoneridge Middle School next academic year. At the meeting, you were able to provide input and raise any questions. A summary of what was presented about the program and discussion highlights are enclosed for you here.

The big decision now is to select the 120 students who will participate in the new program. Please decide if you would like your child to be in the program next year. Indicate your permission on the enclosed application, and mail it to the school by May 1 in the envelope provided. Please do not give the form to your child to bring to school.

If more than 120 students are nominated for inclusion, a committee consisting of five parents who serve on the planning team will conduct an impartial lottery for the selection. By June 1, you will be notified if your child will be in the program.

Sincerely,

Joan Stefans, Principal

P.S.: About ten days before school starts in the fall, all participating students will be asked to come to school for two days. The purpose will be to complete "pretests" in reading, writing, and mathematics. The results will determine at what places each student should start individual study, so he or she can attain satisfactory learning for entering high school.

DETERMINING PARENTS' PRESENT ATTITUDES TOWARD THE SCHOOL

Shortly after June 1, the parents of the selected students are notified by mail. Both Nancy's and Bobby's parents are informed that their children are to be in the new program. Included with the letter is an opinion questionnaire that parents are asked to complete and return. Its purpose is to gather their present feelings about the conventional school program as now conducted. To determine parent attitudes toward the new program, the questionnaire will be repeated after the new program is completed for the first time. Comparisons of the two sets of opinions will be made. Sample questions are shown below. ◆

Sample Attitudinal Questions

1. What do you feel to be your child's motivation level to attend school each day? (mark the line below)

LOW	MODERATE	HIGH

Comments:

2. How well is your child now learning all school subjects?

POORLY	SATISFACTORILY	VERY WELL

Comments:

3. How do you rate your child's learning in each subject (circle a word):

English	LOW	MODERATE	HIGH
Math	LOW	MODERATE	HIGH
History and Geography	LOW	MODERATE	HIGH
Science	LOW	MODERATE	HIGH
Other classes	LOW	MODERATE	HIGH

Comments:

4. How much personal help does your child receive from his or her teachers?

LITTLE	SOME	A LOT

Comments:

5. How well do you believe your child is being educated now in basic subjects of reading, writing, and math?

POORLY	SATISFACTORILY	VERY WELL

Comments:

6. How well is your child prepared for high school?

POORLY	SATISFACTORILY	VERY WELL

Comments:

7. Beyond learning basic subject content, how well is your child being prepared to become a responsible adult in our society?

POORLY	SATISFACTORILY	VERY WELL

Comments:

CHAPTER 24

Preparing Students for the Program

Two weeks before school starts, parents are notified that on August 28 and 29, students chosen for the new program are to meet in the school cafeteria at 8:30 a.m. for pretesting sessions. School buses will make pickups at regular stops and return from school at 12:15 p.m. To encourage attendance, each child will receive a free matinee movie ticket to one of three popular age-appropriate films showing locally. At the principal's request, the theater owners cooperate by supplying tickets.

PRETESTING PROCEDURE

On August 28, students meet with their four new program teachers. Ms. Lopez welcomes them and describes the purpose for pretesting in basic-skills subjects. It is to determine each student's present level of skills that comprise competencies in reading, writing, and mathematics. It is carefully explained that this is not a series of tests to be graded. The results will determine what specific help is needed and where the instruction should start for each individual. The goal is for each student to reach or exceed the competencies established for eighth graders at the end of the school year.

Using the overhead projector, Ms. Lopez shows sample questions and points out the three letters along the right margin for each objective-type question. After answering, the student is to mark whether he or she is **Sure**, **N**ot sure, or has **G**uessed at the answer.

This will help the teacher when analyzing results and making recommendations to the student for study. (See the sample questions on pages 134–135.)

Today's testing is on mathematics and some language arts skills. Tomorrow, the test will be on reading and writing. While students have until noon to complete the test, it is expected that everyone will finish before then. Students can return home or wait on the playground for the bus to arrive at 12:15 p.m. When each student completes the second pretest on the following day, he or she will receive the selected movie ticket. Finally, Ms. Lopez informs them that when they start school in two weeks, each student will receive his or her pretest results. Teachers will schedule meetings with students to review the results.

During the next two weeks, the four teachers work together to evaluate pretest results, prepare an individual profile for each student, and recommend modules for studying necessary basic skills.

ORIENTING STUDENTS
TO THE NEW PROGRAM

This is the first day of the new fall school term. After talking with her parents about the meeting they attended, Nancy—eager to get back to school after the summer—seems excited about the new program. She is curious about how she did on the pretests.

(Continued on page 136)

Sample Pretest Questions

Answer each question, then circle **S** if you are sure, **N** if you are not sure, or **G** if you are guessing.

RECALL

1. In each set, put an **X** before the word that is **NOT** in alphabetical order.　　　S　N　G

   a. _____ chatter　　**b.** _____ candle

      _____ drum　　　　　_____ crack

      _____ angel　　　　　_____ cheese

      _____ guess　　　　　_____ class

      _____ magic　　　　　_____ compare

      　　　　　　　　　　_____ contact

2. Correct each misspelled word.　　　S　N　G

   a. driveing _____　　**e.** a science principal _____

   b. beievable _____　　**f.** pricede _____

   c. hillyest _____　　**g.** familiar _____

   d. receive _____　　**h.** unnecessary _____

3. Solve each problem.　　　S　N　G

   a. $671 - 48$ = _____

   b. $754 + 1236 + 25$ = _____

   c. 548×23 = _____

   d. 1/5 of 50 = _____

   e. 24% of 654 = _____

COMPREHENSION

4. In words, write the number 42,034.　　　S　N　G

_____

5. Use the provided protractor to measure the angle below. It has _____ degrees.　　　S　N　G

6. Put an **X** before the clue that tells you what vowel sound to try in the underlined word.　　　S　N　G

Our neighbor has a <u>cute</u> baby boy.

   _____ a. vowel letter followed by a consonant and final **e**

   _____ b. **o** followed by **Id** or **It**

   _____ c. vowel letter followed by **r**

7. For each sentence, <u>underline</u> the subject and draw a box around the predicate.   S   N   G

    a. Monarch butterflies migrate each year.

    b. I like short stories.

    c. Photography is Betty's main interest.

8. Read the story on the next page, then answer the following three questions.

    a. The main idea of the story is: S   N   G

        _____ The benefits of finding gold may not last.

        _____ Only greedy people seek gold.

        _____ Everyone who seeks gold should find it.

    b. The hero of the story is: S   N   G

        _____ Casey

        _____ Guenther

        _____ Thomas

    c. List three details that support the story's main idea: S   N   G

APPLICATION

9. On the back of this sheet of paper, make a bar graph to illustrate this data: S   N   G

Team	Number of Wins
A	7
B	12
C	4
D	10

10. If it takes 15 seconds to inflate a balloon with compressed air, how many balloons can be inflated in 12 minutes? _____   S   N   G

11. Write the following sentence as an equation: S   N   G

    Four times a number plus negative three is negative nine. _____

12. Solve the following problem. If there is no solution, explain why.   S   N   G

    On a trip of 210 km, Jeff traveled by train for 3 hours and then by bus for the rest. The average train speed was 15 km/hr more than that of the bus. Find the average speed of the bus.

13. On the back of this sheet of paper, write a note of 30 to 50 words congratulating a friend for being elected president of the Student Council.   S   N   G

After a summer on the streets, Bobby is not very impressed with being in the new program. He still views school as an obstacle to the "free" life he experiences on the street with his buddies, but his mother thinks he should be in the program. He frowns after thinking what the results will be on his pretests.

Mrs. Stefans, the principal, starts the meeting with all students in the cafeteria by welcoming them. She reintroduces the four teachers with whom they will study, and then states, "Together we are about to start a very exciting and challenging school year. You will learn new ways of studying, and I am sure will have many worthwhile experiences. Your cooperation and efforts are essential for success. Now let your teachers tell you about the new program."

Each teacher briefly explains a component of the program, as was done at the parents' meeting the previous spring, but presented on a level understandable by the students. Principal Stefans ends the meeting by reiterating the important features of the new program:

- Instruction will be flexible, with no conventional six-period days and changing bells.

- Education will be a mixture of self-directed learning for each student or small groups; teacher presentations of subject-content themes with follow-up group activities; and problem-based projects for group work.

- Teachers will guide and counsel individual students more carefully than they had done during conventional teaching.

- Parents, high school and college students, and other assistants will help teachers and guide students by tutoring them and coordinating their group activities.

- Students will have opportunities to show more initiative and must assume more responsibility for their own learning.

- Evaluation of student learning will be based largely on their accomplishing specific learning objectives in basic skills and subject-content themes, and also on their cooperation, initiative, and individual performance in group activities.

As students take a break, they are quiet and seem thoughtful. Many are confused with all the new things they heard, feeling somewhat uncertain about what lies ahead. But there is also an undercurrent of excitement that sets a high level of anticipation.

When the students go to their assigned homerooms, assistants are introduced and their roles are explained. Then a schedule sheet (like the sample below) that shows the components of the new program is distributed.

A notation on each sheet informs the student which of the two large groups he or she has been

Schedule			
		GROUP A	**GROUP B**
8:15 a.m.	Homeroom		
8:35 a.m.	Period 1	Basic Skills	Interdisciplinary Theme
9:45 a.m.	Break		
10:00 a.m.	Period 2	Interdisciplinary Theme	Basic Skills
11:10 a.m.	Elective		
12:00 p.m.	Lunch		
12:45 p.m.	Period 3	Basic Skills	Project
1:55 p.m.	Period 4	Project	Basic Skills
3:05 p.m.	End School Day		

Sample schedule sheet

assigned to—Group A or Group B. The schedule includes the following:

- Each student has two basic-skills study periods per day, requiring the use of the four regular classrooms.

- The interdisciplinary theme period includes the teacher-presentation phase in the auditorium (30 minutes or so in length, repeated once) with small-group follow-up activities in areas of the cafeteria.

- Elective classes (physical education, health, art, foreign language, etc.) are conducted by other teachers in their rooms.

- Group meetings and activities for problem-solving projects take place in available school space, since students may be using the library or going into the community at various times.

As the school term proceeds and students develop satisfactory competencies in basic skills, teachers will decide whether to reduce the amount of time devoted to basic-skills learning from two to one period per day, as shown in the schedule. Then more group project time may be required, or a second interdisciplinary theme would be started. The latter would permit more time to be devoted to teaching content in academic subjects.

PRETEST RESULTS

At the end of the student orientation meeting, the teachers distribute a profile summary of individual pretest results to each student. The following categories are included:

Language Arts	Mathematics
Mechanics	Arithmetic
Composition	Concepts
Reading	Geometry
	Algebra

The results indicate each student's present competency levels in the many facts, concepts, principles, and skills that comprise the middle school curriculum for basic skills. Ms. Lopez explains the format of a profile and the meaning of the results. (See the two examples included in this chapter.) The left-hand column lists all topics included in the eighth-grade curriculum, plus advanced topics appropriate for study by eighth graders. Next to each topic is a bar indicating the level of pretest results for that student.

Then Ms. Lopez calls attention to the modules for study as shown to the right of subjects for each profile. Modules are indicated for use to overcome deficiencies or for advanced study. Three types are listed with a module number.

- **P**—printed materials (generally worksheets and textbook)

- **AV**—audiotape or videotape recording with text and/or worksheets

- **CS**—computer software

For most topics, students have a choice of the module format for study. Some students may even find it valuable to study the topic in more than one module format. The right-hand column contains blank lines for marking the approval of each topic the student studies. Either the teacher or an assistant must sign off when the student satisfactorily completes the module post-test. These profile sheets become the student's own record of progress to share with parents. The teachers maintain a separate record as a computer file. (Also see the map of modules in Figure 8 on page 79.)

The students examine their profiles. They are told that during the next week, each one will meet with a teacher at the scheduled time noted on the form to review the profile and ask any questions.

Portions of the profile summaries in math and language arts for Bobby and Nancy are shown on page 138. ◆

Pretest Knowledge and Skills Profile   **Student:** BOBBY HESTER

Mathematics

ARITHMETIC	BELOW	8TH GR.	ABOVE	MODULES	APPROV/DATE
1. Addition					
2. Subtraction					
3. Decimals				P5,AV5,CS5	
4. Fractions				P6,AV6,CS6	

CONCEPTS					
8. Ratio & Prop.				P8,AV8,CS8	
9. Graphs					

GEOMETRY					
12. Formulas				P12,AV12,CS12	
13. Angles					

Language Arts

MECHANICS					
1. Spelling				P23,AV23,CS23	
2. Punctuation				P23,AV23,CS23	

COMPOSITION					
9. Vocabulary					
10. Composition				P31,AV31,CS31	
etc. . . .					

Pretest Knowledge and Skills Profile   **Student:** NANCY MARTIN

Mathematics

ARITHMETIC	BELOW	8TH GR.	ABOVE	MODULES	APPROV/DATE
1. Addition					
2. Decimals					
3. Fractions				P6,AV6,CS6	
4. Percentage					

CONCEPTS					
8. Exponents					
9. Estimation				P12,AV12,CS12	
10. Statistics				P13,AV13,CS13	

GEOMETRY					
14. Angles					
17. Formulas				P17,AV17,CS17	

Language Arts

MECHANICS					
28. Nouns					
32. Modifiers				P32,AV32,CS32	
35. Prep. & Conj.				P35,AV35,CS35	

COMPOSITION					
38. Dictionary Use					
39. Writing Paragraphs				P39,AV39,CS39	
40. Writing Letters				P40,AV40,CS40	
etc. . . .					

CHAPTER 25

Participating in Basic Subject Skills Learning

Once the students have received their individual pretest results, they are ready to start their studies in basic skills.

DESCRIPTION OF MODULES

Ms. Lopez points out that the term "module" is defined as a learning package for study by each student, as specified on the individual's profile sheet. She describes the nine design features listed on page 49.

STUDY PROCEDURE

Ms. Lopez discusses the alternative methods of study available to students:

- Self-paced, using a module individually

- Small group (two to three students), cooperatively studying a module together, at times with an aide present

- Individual tutoring by an adult or older student, by request or through teacher counseling

Each student has a choice for the method of study. If necessary, more than one method can be used for repeated study of the topic, following advice of a teacher.

The meeting with each student concludes with this information:

- Location of module packages for use: math in room 14; language arts modules 1–35 in room 18; remaining language arts modules in room 19.

- How to obtain assistance for counseling and answering questions, request tutoring help, sign up for group study, or obtain the teacher's post-test for a module.

- Importance of completing the self-check review in each module to determine one's readiness for the post-test or need for any restudy.

- What to do if a satisfactory level of learning is not attained on the post-test. (Additional forms of post-tests are available for retesting after restudy of problem areas.)

- Times during the day when module study should take place, according to the schedule for each group.

- The need to set one's own work schedule by studying in school and at home.

COUNSELING STUDENTS

Bobby Hester

Bobby looks over his profile sheet. He sees that many of his lines are below the eighth-grade level. He is aware that he doesn't know as much as other students know, but he is surprised to see his weakness in so many things. "Man, it's discouraging," he thinks to himself.

When he meets with Ms. Lopez, she says, "Let's first talk about your math abilities. This profile gives you a good overall picture of your strengths and weaknesses in important math skills. You have satisfactory performance in many fundamentals, but you need improvement and upgrading in a number of topics."

Bobby sits quietly, a dejected look on his face.

"But Bobby," she continues, "we want to help you raise these levels. Whatever you plan to do in the future—high school, then college or a job—will require you to be competent in these fundamentals. You can do it. You have the ability."

"But gosh, it's a lot of work," comments Bobby.

"It looks like that now," replies Ms. Lopez. "But once you get started, it'll surprise you how fast you can move along."

"I don't have to study this stuff all by myself, do I?" asks Bobby. "You said in class we could get help."

"That's right," says Ms. Lopez. "The modules listed for each topic are the materials you should use. Remember, there are different types: printed, audio or video recordings with booklets, and computer programs. If you'd like to meet with other students to study together, write your name on the sheet for that topic posted on the bulletin board. When three or four students have signed up, we'll get you all together with someone who can help you. Then, if you need more help, you can ask for a high school or college student to give you further assistance."

"Hey, that sounds pretty good!" exclaims Bobby.

"Bobby, notice that more than one form of module is listed for each topic. Select the one you'd like to use. You may even want to study two of them on a topic. It can strengthen your learning. Then, as you successfully complete each module, have it signed and dated. Go slowly, but keep moving. Watch your progress and improvements. I'll be monitoring your work as you move ahead."

"OK. I'll get at it," says Bobby seriously. "Where should I start?"

"That's up to you. I know you are interested in science. Math may be a good subject, since it is fac-tual and supports science. But don't let reading or writing get pushed aside. You might start with something like fractions and then go to decimals, where your scores were little lower. Then shift to reading or writing for a while.

"And here's another suggestion to help you study. Add to the list of modules you are to complete an additional one on study skills . . . it's a video . . . special number V6. There are various ways to make your use of study time more productive, and I think this video will help you."

"OK," concludes Bobby. "I'll get to work."

Ms. Lopez adds, "Remember, someone will always be in the room if you need more explanations. You can do it. Let me know if you run into any difficulties."

Bobby looks at his list of modules in math. He glances at the room clock, realizing he has some time now to start working.

Nancy Martin

Nancy reviews her math profile sheet and looks over the list of modules she is to complete. She notices that she has a choice of modules that includes computer software programs for each topic. She prefers this, since she likes the freedom to make decisions for herself and also recognizes the advantages of working with computers.

When Nancy meets Ms. Lopez, the latter commends her for the good learning she shows in most basic topics and then states: "I know you won't stand aside but will push ahead with new learning. As your math profile shows, you need to strengthen yourself in some concepts, then move into algebra topics."

"Yes, I'd like to work on them," replies Nancy.

"The modules are available for you to check out," states Ms. Lopez. "The computer programs include many on CD-ROM. I think you'll enjoy using their multimedia features. You may want to study with Tom Simons and Mary Stein in Mrs. Starr's group. They will probably be ready for much of the same work."

"Sounds good," explains Nancy. "I like to share things when I study new material. Can I take some computer programs home to use?"

"Sure, if your computer will handle them," answers Ms. Lopez. "Be sure to look over the language arts topics on your list. There are some you might want to study, even though your knowledge is already on the eighth-grade level. This can reinforce your strengths."

"I'll do that," states Nancy.

"Be sure to keep a record of your work on your profile chart, as I showed in class. Good luck. I'll be watching your progress," concludes Ms. Lopez.

BOBBY'S PROGRESS

Bobby starts his math study with fractions. From the assistant in Mr. Brown's room, he asks for module AV6, which consists of an audiotape and a short workbook. With it, he is given an audiocassette player with headphones. He signs for the module and the equipment.

Using the audio tutorial program

Bobby goes to a study station at the back of the room. He is curious about it, as he has never used an audiotape for study by himself. He attaches the player, inserts the cassette, and opens his workbook, which instructs him to start the tape. The tape introduces the topic of fractions, specifies what will be learned, and tells Bobby to stop the tape to complete a short pretest on basic arithmetic skills. When he again starts the tape, he hears the answers to the pretest questions. If any are wrong, he is told that he may want to review other modules on any skills in which he has a weakness.

As Bobby progresses through the tape, he is introduced to fractions and their components, how to simplify fractions, how to reduce fractions, and so on. He follows the explanations on tape by looking at diagrams in "frames" in the workbook. Sometimes he is directed to write numbers or make a calculation as the voice pauses. In some spots, he doesn't clearly understand an explanation or an answer. He then rewinds the tape and listens again. He moves along as rapidly or as slowly as he finds necessary.

Periodically he is directed to stop the tape and complete a drill or practice exercise. Feedback is provided immediately. As each concept is concluded, Bobby completes a self-check exercise on all content to that point. Bobby feels very confident about his learning as he concludes the program. He asks an assistant for the post-test on fractions. After Bobby completes the post-test, the assistant checks his answers against the answer key—and Bobby gets a grade of over 90 percent. The assistant reviews with him the two questions he answered wrong. One answer was just an arithmetic mistake, and he now understands the answer for the other missed question. She signs her name and writes the completion data on the line in his profile chart.

This was more concentrated study effort than Bobby had ever made before, and he feels pretty good about the results. Bobby becomes more confident that he can learn successfully by himself. This leads to more interest and enthusiasm, as he selects the next module for study.

At his next study session, Bobby gets AV5 to study decimals. By now, he is comfortable with this method of self-paced learning, yet he recalls the suggestions Ms. Lopez gave him to go over the study skills video. He will do this, but he says to himself, "I really can learn this stuff if it is explained slowly in small pieces, and I like to check myself as I go along."

Because he had some difficulty with decimals, after completing the AV5 module, Bobby decides to check out P5, the printed module on decimals, and take it home for a review.

Using computer software

When Bobby is ready to study the geometry category, he decides to use a software program and accompanying kit for shapes and forms. Another student, Anne, is also ready to study the same topic. They obtain the package that contains a program disk along with a kit of materials. They go to a computer to work together.

After introducing the common geometric shapes, the program explains how geometric figures are constructed, manipulated, and transformed. Relationships among various shapes are shown and described. Bobby particularly likes the use of animation with illustrations in realistic perspective as abstractions are visualized for each concept.

Throughout the presentation, the two students have to interact by responding on the keyboard, using the mouse, or handling the plastic shapes in the kit. Bobby particularly likes the part of the review in which he has to assign the name of a geometric shape to various real objects and structures. The whole thing is really fun!

The two students work together pretty well, although they have some disagreements that are resolved peacefully as they move along. Bobby even explains a couple of concepts to Anne to clarify some points. He is pleased with his participation activity because he feels it strengthens his own learning.

As Bobby thinks about how he is learning on his own, he prefers the more dynamic format of computer programs as compared with the audiotape modules he has used. But he recognizes that the number of available computers is limited, so frequently he may have to use the printed materials and tape recordings.

Group study

Also, Bobby puts his name on a sheet for group study in language arts composition topics. Mr. Larson tells him that he can join two other students to form a study group supervised by a college student. They use modules in print form that guide them through writing paragraphs, compositions, and letters.

As they study the textbook chapters and complete worksheet activities, the students discuss answers within the group; they then outline their plans and share their writings. The college student provides explanations, makes corrections, and offers other guidance. Mr. Larson visits the group to observe their activities and progress.

Bobby likes this cooperative way of learning. While he has to keep up with the activities specified in the modules, he willingly participates, feeling more secure in this small group than he had last year in regular classes. "Gosh," he thinks, "I'm really starting to understand how to write something so that anyone can understand it, if I use this grammar stuff correctly." He feels the hard work is starting to show good results.

In this way, using the various modules and getting help as he needs it, Bobby proceeds to bring his competencies in basic skills up to the requirements specified for the eighth grade. He brags at home about what and how he is learning. His mother catches his enthusiasm and changed interest in school. "Whatever they are doing," she thinks, "is right for Bobby. I'm glad he's in this new program."

NANCY'S PROGRESS

Nancy decides to start with the algebra topic of real numbers. She checks out the CD-ROM with booklet CS19, but does not find a free computer for her immediate use. She talks with the students now using them and finds one that will be free in about a half hour. She places a note on the side partition to reserve the station.

Using a printed module

In the meantime, she looks over her profile sheet and decides to review exponents, for which her rating was relatively low. She selects the printed module that requires the use of a textbook and seats herself at a desk in the room. Rather than following the linear sequence to read a page or two of text, then answer one or more questions, solve problems, and then check answers, she reads through all the content of the chapter. Then Nancy turns to the questions and problems in the accompanying printed material. She feels she can handle them satisfactorily. She completes the self-check test, checks her answers, and finds that she has missed three of them. Before going back to see why she answered them incorrectly, the computer becomes available to her. Nancy decides to return to the printed module later.

Using computer software

The booklet packaged with the CD-ROM informs her how to start her study of real numbers. The software disk is correlated with her math textbook. The program includes a mix of verbal explanations, diagrams, even illustrative photographs, and problem-solving strategies. A number of drill-and-practice exercises are included. Nancy particularly likes the deductive reasoning procedure she must use periodically to reach a decision. Soon she is deeply involved and becomes annoyed when she must stop because it is time to attend the academic theme class. When she returns the software package, she arranges to check it out that afternoon and take it home.

That evening Nancy spends an hour or so on the computer program. During part of the time that she works with the software, her father sits with her and goes through the content himself. It recalls for him the math he had learned from a textbook years ago. He remarks, "This is so much more interesting than math was when I was your age. It's certainly a dynamic way of studying. Education can be so different today."

The computer program ends with a clever educational game that Nancy plays with her brother. He told her he knew a lot about real numbers, but she wins the game! She feels that by going through this program, she is getting a mental workout. The next day, after receiving a high grade on the module post-test, she is confident that she has learned the content completely.

Nancy proceeds to additional software modules in algebra and finds other programs that help her to review mechanics in language arts. As suggested by Ms. Lopez, Mary Stein and Tom Simons join her in some study sessions. They like the explanations, discussions, and even some arguments they share while working together. They all benefit from these learning experiences. Nancy obtains approval signatures for the modules completed. She is pleased to show the results at home, especially after success with the advanced materials in algebra.

FUTURE APPLICATIONS OF BASIC SKILLS

It is important to reinforce the learning students have achieved in their basic skills. At Stoneridge Middle School, this is done in two ways. First, twice during the year, students are retested on those topics originally rated as low in their individual profiles. If a student fails any of these reviews, then modules need to be restudied or tutorial help given.

Second, as students engage in activities in the other two program components—interdisciplinary theme study and problem-based projects—they will have many opportunities to apply the knowledge and skills they acquire in reading, writing, and mathematics. For example, see the work with math formulas on pages 148–149 and with decimals on page 161 that Bobby must apply in the theme and group projects. ◆

CHAPTER 26

Participating in an Interdisciplinary Theme Study

On the second day of the new term, the interdisciplinary schedule for Groups A and B starts (see periods 1 and 2 in the schedule on page 136). Each group of students meets at the assigned time in the school auditorium.

INITIATING A THEME

Mr. Brown and Mrs. Starr stand at the front. The instructional theme is "Travel through the Atmosphere and Space." Mrs. Starr explains that this theme includes topics and subject content in four academic areas. She projects a transparency (shown below).

Mr. Brown states that although science is the primary subject area, content in three other major areas relate to the science concepts noted on the transparency. It will take up to six presentation sessions (30 minutes each) plus small-group activities or follow-up study to accomplish the objectives for the theme.

PRETEST

First, the students take a brief science pretest. Its purpose is to determine how many important terms as used in this theme are understood by the students. Some of these terms should have been learned in previous grades.

Bobby grimaces, since he doesn't like this pretest business. He feels it shows his ignorance. But the other students won't see his scores, so he decides it's

---

Travel through the Atmosphere and Space

SCIENCE	**MATH**
Force and Motion	Using Formulas
Acceleration and Velocity	Graphing Time/Distance
Newton's Laws	
Principles of Flight	**LANGUAGE ARTS**
Principles of Space Travel	Literature— Flight/Space
	Biography— Early Aviators
SOCIAL STUDIES	Inventors
History of Flight and Space Travel	Space Explorers

okay. Nancy views the pretest as a challenge. It's sort of fun, she feels, to find out what she already knows about a topic and then to identify the new material she should learn.

The first five questions of the pretest for Stoneridge students are shown at right.

When Mrs. Starr collects the completed pretests, she tells the students they will receive their results tomorrow. (The pretests are then graded by two aides.) Again, students are reminded that this pretest is only an indication of what each one now knows. It helps the teachers to decide what content may need special attention in their presentations. It also gives students an idea of some of the important concepts they will be studying.

Pretest Questions

Match the term on the left by writing its number next to the letter of the definition on the right.

1. Acceleration	_____	a. the air resistance that makes an aircraft fly
2. Inertia	_____	b. change in position compared to a starting point
3. Lift	_____	c. change in speed of an object over time
4. Motion	_____	d. resistance to change in motion
5. Speed	_____	e. distance covered in a period of time

and so on . . .

LEARNING OBJECTIVES

Then Mrs. Starr distributes a list of the learning objectives to be treated in the theme. It includes these:

1. Identify the characteristics of force and describe its relationship to motion.

2. Compare and contrast acceleration, velocity, and speed.

3. Describe the characteristics of the forces that cause flight in the atmosphere and in space.

4. Use Newton's Laws of Motion to solve problems involving motion.

5. Demonstrate Bernoulli's principle of flight, including lift, thrust, and drag.

6. Apply math formulas to measure four physical effects and motions with 80 percent accuracy.

7. Identify at least five persons who contributed to early flight and space explorations, and describe their accomplishments.

FIRST GROUP SESSION

Mr. Brown informs the students they now are to meet in small groups in the cafeteria. A letter written on their pretest sheets assigns each individual to one of 10 groups, each consisting of 6 or 7 students. As students settle at their assigned tables, Mrs. Starr tells them their first job is to select individuals to fill certain responsibilities.

Roles and responsibilities

Within each student group, four roles must be filled:

- The *leader* will coordinate assigned activities and chair meetings during the theme study.

- The *recorder* will take notes during meetings.

- The *timekeeper* will keep the group on task during assigned time periods.

- The *reporter* will coordinate progress reports along with the leader and recorder.

When the next theme starts, other students will fill these roles on a rotating basis. Thus, throughout the year, all students will have an opportunity to fulfill each responsibility one or more times.

Bobby is assigned to group C, along with five other students. They know each other only casually. After introducing themselves, they vote for their first leader. Bobby is elected! This comes as a surprise, and he is uncertain about what to do. Mr. Brown is nearby, and he suggests that Bobby first ask the group to choose a person to be the recorder.

Introductory activity

Once the groups have chosen their leaders and filled the other positions, Mrs. Starr gets all groups started on an introductory activity. She asks that within the remaining 20 minutes of the period, each group answer these questions relating to the theme of "Travel through the Atmosphere and Space":

1. What do you **think** and **feel** about the theme?

2. What do you now **know** about the theme?

3. Are there things you would **like to learn** about the theme?

The purposes for these questions are to motivate a discussion about the theme and to reveal any general misconceptions students may have. Each group is given a large sheet of paper to record answers. They will present their responses to the whole class tomorrow.

Gradually, Bobby assumes his leadership role. It's different from just talking with his friends on the street, he realizes! You really have to stay alert and work at this! Both a democratic approach and some firmness must be used. You have to make decisions. Slowly he learns, and by the end of the period, he starts to feel comfortable.

Nancy is just a participant in her group. But she offers good suggestions for the wording of answers to be shown to the class. She also corrects spelling errors on the display paper they are preparing.

FIRST CLASS SESSION

The next day, the students meet in the auditorium for their theme study periods. First they receive their pretest results. Neither Nancy nor Bobby has more than four of the twelve definitions correct, about average for the class.

Then each group leader presents answers to the three questions introduced the previous day. Mr. Brown and Mrs. Starr commend the groups for their expressed interest in the theme. The teachers also call attention to incorrect answers like those below, which will be corrected during instruction:

- Gravity holds an airplane in the sky.

- Acceleration is another word for velocity.

- Inertia causes a moving object to slow down and stop.

- An airplane stays aloft only because of the action of the propeller or jet engine.

Instructional activities

To illustrate the theme, the video *Aerodynamics of Flight* is shown. It illustrates how kites, gliders, airplanes, and rockets can move through the atmosphere and space. Mrs. Starr tells the class that the video will be shown in its entirety. Then, because it contains illustrations and explanations of many complex concepts, the video will be viewed again. This time, Mrs. Starr will stop it after each new concept is presented, and she will ask for questions from the students. (This technique will reinforce the information.) Using this procedure, the teachers feel that students can better understand the concepts of how various objects accomplish their flight, and students should grasp the meaning of new vocabulary terms described through the visualizations.

At the conclusion of the video, Mrs. Starr tells the students that an understanding of the principles illustrated can be developed by answering the following questions:

- When does a force produce motion?

- What force causes objects to fall?

- How does weight affect gravitational force?

- What is inertia?

- How is velocity related to acceleration?

and so on . . .

The students receive a list of all the questions. For homework, they are to read Unit Six in their science textbooks, which relates to content for the questions, and to look for connections among these concepts. Students are to be prepared to discuss answers in their small groups tomorrow.

Both Nancy and Bobby like the way Mrs. Starr handled this class. Repeating the video was very helpful in following along and understanding the ideas presented. And receiving copies of the questions was much better than having to copy them on paper. Both students know what is required of them for homework. With a good learning start, Bobby looks forward to answering the questions.

SECOND GROUP SESSION

When the students settle into their groups in the cafeteria on the following day, they prepare to discuss their answers to the homework questions. The recorder for each group gets a sheet of transparency film and a felt pen from the supply table. Answers to two assigned questions, once agreed upon in the group, are to be written on the film.

Activities

The two teachers circulate among the groups, offering help and encouraging participation. After the 20-minute group discussion period, Mrs. Starr asks each group leader to present his or her group's answers to their assigned questions. There are some differences, and students discuss them. The teachers clarify any incorrect understanding and poor wording. Then they compliment the groups for their good work.

Finally, the students are given a worksheet to complete for homework that contains descriptions of episodes that apply the concepts in the questions that have been studied and answered. They are to identify the concepts being applied. A rereading of the text chapter might be helpful, they are told.

That afternoon after school, Mrs. Starr and Mr. Brown together review the activities for the theme so far. They realize that they might be moving ahead too rapidly for some students, so they decide to limit the number of concepts to be treated at one time and to reinforce the learning, as was done today.

THIRD GROUP SESSION

The worksheet answers are discussed in the small groups and summarized in the class the next day. For homework, the students are directed to read in their texts about Newton's Laws and Bernoulli's principle of flight, and to complete a worksheet that summarizes these concepts in preparation for tomorrow's teacher presentation. At the end of this session, the students are given a schedule of conventional classes in supplemental subjects they are to attend (art, drama, physical education, health, foreign languages, and so forth). For the next period, they proceed to these classes.

SECOND CLASS SESSION

Demonstrations

When students meet for their whole-class theme period the next day, they see that Mr. Brown has set up a number of demonstrations to illustrate Newton's Laws and Bernoulli's principle. Each student is to inspect the demonstrations and classify each one under the headings of Newton's 1st, 2nd, or 3rd Laws, or Bernoulli's principle. After discussion with the students, Mr. Brown prepares to show a Level 1 interactive videodisc on Newton's Laws and aircraft flight.

Videodisc Use

The disc contains a number of chapters illustrating the action of a force or other effect on an object, aircraft, or space vehicle. Then a question appears on the screen concerning the reaction that may take place. A choice of two or three possible answers is offered. The students are asked to raise their hands to vote on the correct answer. Based on the selected answer, Mr. Brown punches in a code on the video remote control. Immediately, a segment plays, showing the resulting reaction according to the chosen answer . . . right or wrong. This becomes a motivating game, and, as the responses show students' answers are frequently correct.

This presentation class continues as Mrs. Starr asks the students to identify the components of force, distance, acceleration, and velocity. This gives them the opportunity to relate the terms to what they have learned, and to discuss their applications, all leading to the formulas:

- force = mass x acceleration
- distance = speed x time
- acceleration = speed change over time
- velocity = acceleration x time

FOURTH GROUP SESSION

In their groups, using the explanations in their science books, students start applying the formulas. Those who have had difficulties with understanding formulas or carrying out calculations can review or improve their abilities in various ways. Bobby had recently studied the self-paced module on math formulas. He works with two members of his group, and they teach each other how to use variables in applying the formulas. Nancy helps another boy in her group. The teacher suggests to a few students that they go back to the basic-skills modules to restudy some fundamental math concepts.

As the students work, the two teachers circulate among the groups, answering questions and providing explanations. Then, after 45 minutes, the students are directed to reassemble in the auditorium.

THIRD CLASS SESSION

Mrs. Starr uses this half hour to review what has been learned so far in the theme. First, she distributes a summary worksheet. Then she goes over the meaning of new terms, including the laws, principles, and math formulas. Students take notes. Mr. Brown informs students that they should look over the objectives for the theme, and review any areas in which they may feel uncertain or weak. In two days, they will be tested on this material.

As Bobby looks over his worksheets, he feels pretty good. He has a good understanding of most material and can review weak areas tonight. Nancy feels secure with the knowledge she has acquired.

FURTHER THEMATIC TEACHING/LEARNING ACTIVITIES AND EVALUATION

As the study of this theme continues, in addition to science topics, other teacher presentations will treat the following:

- graphing time and distance problems
- the history of flight
- the development of space travel
- the literature of flight and space travel (poetry, novels, biographies, nonfiction)

The teachers use a variety of media resources, and even arrange for an amplified telephone conversation with a NASA official during which students can ask questions about space flight and future plans, including the space platform that is to be operated in cooperation with Russia and other nations.

In small-group activities and for homework, in addition to activities related to teacher presentations, students can:

- investigate the kinds of forces and motion used in a number of different sports (baseball, football, tennis, sailing)

- develop ways to calculate speed, acceleration, and velocity while moving on a bicycle, car, rollerblades, and skateboard

- calculate the velocity of various balls thrown against a wall (tennis ball, softball, baseball, basketball, soccer ball)

- study selected biographies (the Wright brothers, Charles Lindberg, Robert Goddard, Amelia Earhart, and so forth), using print resources, CD-ROM references, and videos available in the school library or borrowed from the public library; then prepare reports and share them in their small groups, after which selections for presentations to the large class are made

- use and report on computer software such as "In Search of Space: Introduction to Rocketry," and "Flight: Aerodynamics of Model Rockets"

- use the Internet to find information about their topics from other libraries and governmental sources

- use e-mail to raise questions and have discussions on their subjects with students elsewhere

- use the Internet to find groups of people already addressing their topics in discussion groups on the Web

- survey and report on potential vocations in aviation and space technology

As indicated, students can select one or more of the above projects. (Some projects may be engaged in by more than one student group.) They gather information and prepare a written report along with a display or a presentation. Several presentations may be offered to the class simultaneously in different rooms. Therefore, students need to publicize their project to attract other students to attend theirs. Presentations are repeated more than once. An example of friendly competition in action!

Finally, as a culminating activity, a paper airplane flying contest is staged. This will involve all students, as individuals or as teams, to design, construct, and then one afternoon to fly their creations on the playground. All students, teachers, and parents attending will judge success on the basis of:

• aesthetic design

• duration of flight

• distance covered from release point

• aerobatic display

Final evaluation of student learning for the theme is based on:

• objective-type and essay tests over learning objectives for subject content

• responsibilities and participation in group activities

• written and oral reports, readings, and other individual or group work

A second theme period is scheduled. The other two teachers on the team, Ms. Lopez and Mr. Larson, are planning a theme with a social studies emphasis. The topic they've chosen is "The Federal Government versus the State Government: What Are the Differences?" ◆

CHAPTER 27

Time for Formative Evaluation

At the end of the first month of the new program's implementation, in consultation with Dr. Lewis, the facilitator, the teachers decide to obtain some preliminary reactions from students about how they feel the new program is going. All students and their four teachers meet in the auditorium.

Students are asked to respond to the following questions on a 1 to 4 scale (1=low to 4=high). The questions are also discussed with them during the general meeting.

---

1. How do you like the new program so far, in comparison to the regular teaching you experienced last year, and why?

2. How do you feel about the amount of daily work assigned?

3. How do you rate the different ways you can study your basic skills? (rate from favorite to least preferred)

   • self-study modules

   • working in groups with other students

   • tutorial help

4. Is the use of themes a good way to study academic subjects?

5. How well does the combination of teacher presentation and follow-up small-group activities hold your interest and provide satisfactory ways to learn?

A brief questionnaire is sent home to parents for their comments about the new program. This is similar to the attitudinal questions originally asked about the conventional program (see page 132).

After students complete their questionnaires, a discussion takes place. Some questions asked and responses made are:

• "I was directed to use self-study modules. I don't think I learn as well when I work alone. Can I work on modules with other students?" (This response shows a misunderstanding on the part of the student, as students may work together on modules. Alternative study methods are also available, including group study.)

• "Will this approach be used in the high school we attend?" (Not at present, to our knowledge.)

• "Can the school get more computers for us to use?" (We are working on this.)

• "I have a close friend in school not in the program. When will his class become involved?" (You are in the first tryout group; we are hoping to expand the program to include other students, probably next year.)

• "I like the different activities we do each day. It's better than sitting in one class after another and listening to the teachers talk." (Thank you.)

• "The way the teachers have organized the parts of the program makes learning more interesting." (We are pleased that you find learning more interesting.)

- "I think we students have too much freedom and responsibility. We should be told more about what we need to learn and [be] directed to do it." (We realize that not all students are comfortable with the approach taken in the new program. If you continue to feel uncomfortable, please talk with your teacher. Together with you, we can decide to let you return to conventional classes. [Note to other teachers in the new program: This student is still locked into Stage 1 of the McBeath model. Close supervision and additional attention may help this student gain confidence.]

- "I like this approach. It's hard for anyone to goof off. You have to be responsible to the group for getting your work done." (Good. That's a perceptive and true observation.)

As this portion of the session ends, the students are informed that next week they will be given a note to invite their parents to a progress report meeting at school.

The teachers and the principal meet to review the replies received from both students and parents. The comments made by students in the general meeting are also considered. All this evidence will help them to revise and strengthen aspects of the new program as it proceeds now and as additional teachers and students become involved. It is noted that the responses are generally very positive. ◆

CHAPTER 28

Participating in the Problem-Based Project

As the first two components of the program (self-directed study in basic skills and interdisciplinary theme study) become established, and students start to feel comfortable with the schedule and instructional activities, it is time to introduce the third component: problem-based learning projects.

INTRODUCTION TO THE PROJECT

At a total group meeting, Mr. Larson tells students that they will work together in groups of five on a project. For now, students will be *assigned* to groups. In future projects, they may be allowed to form their own groups. Each group will have an adult coordinator. Mr. Larson then uses the overhead projector and defines a project with this transparency:

> A project is a topic, a problem, or an issue that is of interest to the group. It may require study and research at school, community contacts, and various activities to investigate, gather information, and reach a conclusion, a decision, or a final product.

He cites examples of possible topics (see page 116). Then he outlines the parameters of the project, distributing to each student a handout that contains the above definition and the procedures to follow.

- Select a group leader and assign other responsibilities (scheduler, record keeper, and so on). These positions should be for the duration of the project.

- Keep a journal or diary of one's activities throughout the project and collect materials prepared in a portfolio (by each student).

- Consider potential topics of interest; discuss and evaluate them, asking these questions: Is this an important topic? Are we all interested in it? Will we be able to gather information and do necessary work in school or in the community? Will we be able to complete our work within the required time (six weeks)?

- Decide what should be accomplished (the objectives).

- Develop and record a plan to carry out the project.

- Set a time schedule for activities.

- Obtain approval from the adult coordinator assigned to the group who will review the plan with a teacher.

- Consult with a teacher as necessary.

- Be prepared to describe the project and plans at a reporting session of all students, to be scheduled in a week or so.

- Delegate and share duties within the group as the project proceeds.

- According to the plan, make contact with school support personnel (library media specialist, other teachers, university students, and so on) and community persons.

- Carry out all activities.

- Analyze and organize the information collected.

- Reach decisions or a conclusion, in answer to the project objectives.

- Prepare a report, exhibit, or media production.

- Make a presentation of the results before all students and invited guests, including parents and especially involved community members who assisted the group.

STARTING THE PROJECT

One project group consists of Nancy Martin, Bobby Hester, Manuel Rodriguez, Lieu Kim, and Sid Grant. Mrs. Lake, a parent, works with the group as coordinator.

At the first group meeting, Mrs. Lake, following the briefing she had received, reviews the items on Mr. Larson's parameter handout. The students follow along, often nodding as they show understanding of what is required. They ask these questions:

- "How long do we have for this project?"

- "What happens if we can't agree on one topic?"

- "Can we get help from high school kids who have done projects like this? I know my brother did something like this."

The questions are discussed, with these answers resulting:

- "Since this is your first experience, six weeks are scheduled."

- "You need to find a topic on which all can agree. This needs to be a problem each person accepts and will cooperate in carrying out."

- "Yes, you can obtain suggestions from other persons, but the group must do the planning and ac-

tual work. Choose a new topic, not one with which any of you are familiar or that has been done by a friend or family member."

Selecting a leader and a record keeper

The activity starts as Mrs. Lake asks who would like to be group leader.

"What does the group leader do?" asks Bobby.

"What do you think the leader should do?" replies Mrs. Lake.

These responsibilities are enumerated by the group:

- Call and conduct meetings

- Make assignments

- Preside when voting is necessary

- Make contacts with suggested resource persons through the coordinator

- Keep the coordinator informed of activities and progress

- Supervise preparation of reports and direct the final presentation, although all team members will be involved

"That's a good start," says Mrs. Lake. "Now, who would like to be the leader?"

"How about you, Sid?" says Manuel.

"Well, if you all want me to do it, okay," replies Sid.

"Would anyone else like to be group leader?" asks Mrs. Lake.

When no student responds, she requests a show of hands for Sid to become group leader. The vote is unanimous.

"How about calling the leader the 'project manager'?" Nancy asks. "It sounds better than 'group leader.'"

"Okay with me," Sid says.

"Now, what other jobs have to be filled?" asks Mrs. Lake.

After a short discussion, it is agreed that for now there is only a need for a record keeper to take notes on discussions and decisions. Other assignments will be made as needs arise. Mrs. Lake suggests that it would be helpful if the record keeper has computer skills, especially word processing. Lieu Kim says she has those skills. The group votes for Lieu as record keeper.

Deciding on a topic

Sid begins his management duties by starting a discussion of potential topics for investigation. The group mentions some topics that Mr. Brown had noted in his introductory talk. Sid asks for ideas from the group, and asks Lieu to start a list on a flipchart. She records the following ideas:

- Use of drugs in the school

- Recycling garbage and waste materials

- Life in a high school

- Eating a nutritious lunch

- Recognizing characteristics of different cultural groups

- Evaluating new computer games

After a discussion of these suggested topics, the group narrows them to the ones about nutritious lunches and computer games. Finally they agree on the subject of nutritious lunches . . . knowing what they get in the school cafeteria each day!

"That sounds pretty broad—a nutritious lunch," says Mrs. Lake. "Can you be more specific?"

"How about comparing our lunch hamburgers with those at McDonald's and other places?" asks Manuel.

"What do you mean, 'comparing them'?" asks Nancy.

"Well, figuring out how good they are . . . like the food value of them," replies Manuel.

"Maybe we could take the same idea, but do it for different pizzas . . . maybe comparing the costs and nutrition, and deciding which one is the best value," explains Sid. "I think pizza may be more fun than looking at hamburgers. All the kids would be interested in what we find out."

"We don't eat pizza at my house," states Nancy. "My dad thinks there's too much cholesterol in the cheese and other ingredients."

"That may be true," replies Lieu. "But so many people do eat them that it could be good to find out which pizza is the best value."

"I agree. That sounds like a good subject," says Bobby. "Could be fun to do . . . and maybe we'll get some pizza to eat!"

"Okay," states Sid. "Let's vote. How many in favor of examining different pizzas?"

All hands go up except Nancy's.

"Let's make sure we clearly state what we want to do," advises Mrs. Lake.

Nancy asks, "How about . . . investigating the nutritional value and cost of pizzas that are sold in our town?"

"I suppose what we should come up with is a rating of the different pizzas for nutrition and cost," says Lieu.

"That sounds okay. A good start. Make sure you have both Nancy's and your own statements on paper, Lieu. That will be what we hope to accomplish," concludes Mrs. Lake. "For tomorrow, let's all think about how we should begin the investigation."

PLANNING THE INVESTIGATION

When the group meets the next day, the first matter is the meaning of the expression "nutritional value." From their science and health classes, the students have some knowledge about carbohydrates, protein, fat, and vitamins in foods. How to determine their value is the question.

Further discussion results in the start of a plan for their investigation. It includes the following:

1. Talk with Mr. Sanchez, the health teacher.

2. Identify local restaurants that sell pizza.

3. Visit a few restaurants and obtain any nutritional information they have.

4. Evaluate the information and see if it is helpful.

5. Buy a small pizza from each store. ("Is money available from school for purchases?") Record the costs.

6. Talk with Mrs. Starr in science about how to analyze the pizzas nutritionally.

7. Do some experiments or analyses.

8. Determine the results.

9. Decide on ratings for the pizzas.

The group agrees that this sounds like a useful plan at this time. Bobby suggests that the name for the project can be "Best Pizza Buy." Everyone agrees this is a good title.

"What happens if we need to change the plan because of something we learn as we move ahead?" asks Manuel. "After we do one thing, we might discover something new that needs to be done."

"Good point," remarks Mrs. Lake. "I'm sure you can modify the plan if there is a good reason. Lieu, why don't you take the planning list you have to Ms. Lopez and ask if you can use a computer to start a file for our project?"

Later that afternoon, Lieu works at a computer to print out the project plan. She makes copies for Mrs. Lake and the other group members. It looks like this:

Project Title: Best Pizza Buy

Purpose: To examine different pizzas sold in our town and rate them according to nutritional value and cost

Plan: [The nine items listed above]

The next day, Mrs. Lake shows the plan to Ms. Lopez, who is responsible for the group. After looking it over, Ms. Lopez approves the plan, agreeing to meet with the group the following day. Mrs. Lake comments that she is enjoying her time with this student group.

The next day, Ms. Lopez goes over the plan with the group, commending them on their planning, and suggesting that they add some library research to learn more about nutritional values in foods and how various values are determined. Also, she tells them that money to cover the cost of purchasing five small pizzas, with the same three toppings, has been approved to spend.

Finally, Ms. Lopez says that she hopes the students are making entries in their personal journals about the work each is doing as the project proceeds.

GATHERING INFORMATION

Sid suggests that they first talk with Mr. Sanchez before doing the library research. He reminds Lieu to add the research activity to their plan. The group concurs, and Sid goes to the school office to check Mr. Sanchez's schedule. He leaves a note asking Mr. Sanchez to come to their meeting place, if possible, when he is out of class in half an hour.

Locating pizza sources

In the meantime, the group looks over the list of pizza restaurants and delivery services that Nancy has prepared from the yellow pages. They are surprised to find there are 17 restaurants that sell pizza in their town. It is agreed that only those that deliver pizza should be included in their study. This limits the number to five.

They decide to obtain the same pizza with the same toppings from each store. After discussion, the students agree that each pizza to be analyzed will contain cheese, pepperoni, and sausage.

Consulting with the health teacher

When Mr. Sanchez meets with the group, he tells them that regulations require that the nutritional values of fast foods, including pizza, be available at the restaurant or place of business. He explains that this information should include calories, protein, carbohydrate, and fat content. In addition, cholesterol, sodium, and even chemicals that may be added for flavor or preservation should be listed. This would give a complete indication of the nutritional value.

Then Mr. Sanchez states that if the group wants more detailed information about nutritional matters, they might want to talk with Dr. Smith in the Foods and Nutritional Science Department at the nearby university. This interests the students. They thank Mr. Sanchez and agree to contact Dr. Smith. He finally suggests that they might want to record on audiotape any information Dr. Smith gives them for use in their study and report.

Library research

In the school library, the students look through the various bound encyclopedias and a couple of new

CD-ROM references, using the terms "nutrition," "food values," and "pizza." They take some notes but do not find much useful information relating directly to their pizza subject. Bobby and Manuel had talked about the meaning of the terms "protein," "carbohydrates," and "fat." They aren't certain about the definitions and decide to look them up in more detail.

Sid talks with Mrs. Sawitz, the library media specialist. She takes them to a computer terminal and shows them how to log on to the city public library database. They use the same key words and find some references in health books and a few magazine articles. The reference titles and sources are printed out. Lieu and Manuel agree to go to the public library after school and read the references.

Before leaving the library, Sid asks if the group can borrow an audio recorder and a blank tape cassette for their meeting with Dr. Smith. This is arranged. Sid asks Bobby to do the recording if they are able to visit with Dr. Smith. Bobby is pleased with this assignment, since he feels competent in using the recorder after his self-paced learning with the tapes.

Consultation with a nutritional expert

Mrs. Lake obtains Dr. Smith's phone number and makes contact with her. The coordinator explains the project and asks Dr. Smith if she would talk with Sid Grant, the student project manager. When Sid makes the call, he explains the purpose for the project and asks if Dr. Smith can advise them on how comparisons can be made among the various pizzas for the nutritional factors that Mr. Sanchez had listed. Dr. Smith suggests that the students come to her laboratory at the university, where she can show them how nutritional values are determined. An appointment is made for two days later at 2:30 p.m.

A visit to the university

Mrs. Lake speaks with Ms. Lopez about arrangements to make the trip to the university. This requires a signed permission from parents and transportation. Mrs. Lake will drive her car, and Nancy says she will ask her mother to drive as well.

The next day, each student brings a signed permission form. Some parents have expressed an interest in what the students are doing in their project. The students are enthused and eager to visit with Dr. Smith. In the meantime, during project time today, the students work on a form they will use while gathering information about the pizza products, including nutritional values and purchase prices. They agree that each student will go to one assigned store on the following Saturday to obtain nutritional data there.

The visit with Dr. Smith starts as Sid asks if they can record the information she gives them. She agrees. Then Dr. Smith explains, as did Mr. Sanchez, that each business must make available the nutritional information about their products.

"How accurate and honest is the information?" asks Nancy.

"It is supposed to be correct. The Department of Health periodically checks on the accuracy. Also, in one of my classes, we conduct laboratory analyses of fast-food products. It pretty well matches what the stores report."

Then Dr. Smith provides the students with this procedure for determining nutritional values:

1. Weigh the pizza.

2. Identify the toppings and type of dough.

3. Look up nutritional content of each ingredient.

4. Separate and weigh each topping ingredient and the dough.

5. Calculate nutritional values by the following formula:

$$\text{Percentage of Pizza's Nutritional Value} = \frac{\text{Grams of Nutritional Content}}{\text{Total Weight of Pizza}}$$

Nancy asks, "Do the same toppings, like cheese or pepperoni, used at different places, all have the same nutritional values?"

"Not necessarily," replies Dr. Smith. "You may want to use a database software program we have. It shows varieties of food products and their nutritional content. This is more detailed and up-to-date than the printed reference I've shown you."

"May we use the software?" questions Sid.

"Sure, I'll give you a copy. It's public domain. We have a number of copies for student use."

"As you find the information you need, you may want to make a table or spreadsheet to record the data," Dr. Smith states. "Then a summary can show food values and relative costs for each product."

Finally, she tells the students they might want to do some research to substantiate what they find. They can examine reference materials in the university library. She'll arrange permission for them. She knows that a number of articles have been written on this subject and published in journals in her field. She gives them some keywords to check and shows them how they can use the computer in her office to search through the university collection and periodicals. Sid tells Dr. Smith about the initial information they found in their research at the public library.

As the visit ends, Dr. Smith gives them her e-mail address and fax number in case they want to communicate further with her. She invites them back whenever they would like to do the library search. Also, she tells them that if their teacher doesn't have the necessary scale for weighing the food samples, equipment can be used in her lab.

The students thank Dr. Smith for the information and for her time. On the way back to school, Lieu remarks, "I'd like to know more about food science. It might be an interesting career."

Bobby adds, "That was good stuff. That's the first time I've seen a real science lab. I'd like to work in a place like that."

"Why don't you go back?" Manuel says. "She told us to visit if we wanted to."

"I think I might," Bobby says seriously. "I could do some of the weighing tests there."

Taking stock of progress

That evening at home, Nancy's mother, who drove some students to and from the university, asks Nancy to tell her father about their pizza project. She describes what they are doing, showing him the project plan and saying, "This is a good way to learn about something. I really don't care about pizzas. Like you, I don't like to eat them. We've heard about the scientific method, but this is the first time I can really see how it works. There's a lot of detail and careful work

involved in gathering information before getting to a conclusion."

"That's good thinking, Nancy," says her dad. "It sounds like this new program you're in is doing okay."

"Yes, Nancy's group all seem to be working hard on their project," adds Mrs. Martin.

It has become a common practice during lunch at school for students to tell each other about their projects. There is a lot of enthusiasm expressed, along with descriptions of activities, and some bragging about how good a group's project will be.

At the next group meeting, Mrs. Lake asks the students to review what they have learned in the visit with Dr. Smith. Lieu reads her notes. Bobby suggests that they listen to the recording that was made, so they can better understand the formula suggested by Dr. Smith for calculating nutritional values.

The students check off the parts of the plan they have completed, adding new items to the list. They agree the following still need to be done:

- Locate and read references found in the public library.

- Check references through the university source.

- Buy pizzas.

- Conduct lab tests, in school or at the university.

- Compile data.

- Determine results.

- Make pizza ratings.

PLANNING THE ANALYSES

The following Saturday, each student visits an assigned store or restaurant and obtains information about nutritional values and prices for the pizza to be purchased. At their next meeting, each one transfers the nutritional information to a chart that Nancy has prepared. Also, Manuel and Lieu report on their readings at the library. They suggest that each student read and take notes on two articles that contain useful information about nutritional values. This will provide students with a common background of understanding.

The group is now prepared to buy their pizzas and do the analyses. Sid talks with Mrs. Starr about doing the tests. She has containers, tools, and a small gram scale. Sid tells the group they may want to contact Dr. Smith to use the larger, more accurate scale at the university.

The next day, a phone call confirms Dr. Smith's agreement that they can do the lab work there. She gives them a choice of times to visit. A procedural plan for the tests is developed. This time, the information is faxed to Dr. Smith. She replies by fax, asking a couple of questions, which the students answer and fax back to Dr. Smith. None of the students has ever seen a fax being sent and replied to so quickly. They are impressed with all these communication technologies.

Near the end of this session, Ms. Lopez comes to the group. She tells them that on the following Monday, each group is to make a 10-minute progress report on their project to all students. They can do it in any suitable way so as to inform other students of their plans and explain what they have accomplished to the present. Also, a report is to be submitted on paper.

REPORTING PROGRESS

The group decides that the next few days should be devoted to preparing the two reports. First, there is disagreement as to whether the written report or group presentation should be developed first. Nancy and Bobby feel that the presentation to the students is more important for the broad impression they can give to all the other students. But the other three members want to do the written report for Ms. Lopez first, since she will give it a grade. Then Nancy reminds them that she is sure the presentation will be graded also.

When the group votes, the majority is in favor of preparing the written report first; from that, they will develop the presentation.

As Sid writes on a flipchart, the group reviews its progress to date. This list of the group's accomplishments then becomes the outline for the written report, which is shown in the box on this page.

The students discuss who should prepare the written material for each of these five items. Since the last three contain the main details to be explained, Sid asks for volunteers.

Outline for Report

Major outcomes for project

Nine-step plan (revised from original plan)

Contacts with Mr. Sanchez and Dr. Smith

Information about five pizzas

Research completed

Preparation for lab analyses

Lieu offers to report on the pizza purchases and summarize the research completed, since she already has notes. Nancy asks if Lieu will give her the notes taken during the meeting with Mr. Sanchez, along with the audiotape from Dr. Smith; she will report on those two meetings. Manuel volunteers to help Nancy.

Bobby reluctantly agrees to write up the plan for analyzing the pizzas. Sid offers to work with him.

The written material

Each student does the agreed writing. Everyone wants this to be a good report, so they don't think of what they will do at home for the project as regular homework. Even Bobby shares his work with his mother. She notices his interest and enthusiasm as he tells her about Dr. Smith and her laboratory.

Two days before the reporting date, the members share their writings, argue points for inclusion or accuracy, and correct some English usage. With each student, Mrs. Lake reviews his or her part of the report. Then Lieu, helped by Manuel, goes to the computer to prepare the report.

As Mrs. Lake reads over the students' writing, she notes many grammatical errors in Sid's work. She shows his portion to Ms. Lopez, who meets with Sid and suggests that he study certain grammar rules, including:

• making subjects and verbs agree

• using compound and complex sentences

Sid agrees that he needs help. He hasn't yet been able to study these basic-skills topics. He really hates to take the time now, but he checks out the necessary self-instructional modules and goes through them.

The presentation

Sid, Bobby, and Nancy work on the report for the group presentation. They decide to use overhead transparencies to show the key points, and to play one minute of Dr. Smith's tape on the analysis procedure. They receive help from a university student in preparing the visual materials.

All members of the group meet together during free time on Monday morning, before the afternoon reports are to be made. Mrs. Lake is with them. They have all the materials ready for the written and verbal reports. The final decision is to determine how each person will participate in the presentation, and to make a trial run, speaking and handling the visuals. They know their time is limited to 10 minutes.

Sid will introduce the project objective and the plan. Nancy will report on the meetings with Mr. Sanchez and Dr. Smith. Lieu will describe the pizzas and summarize the evidence from research. Bobby and Manuel will describe how the analyses will be carried out. Sid will conclude the report.

Bobby suggests they could end with a contest to see who in the class can guess which pizza, with what nutritional values, will come out as the most nutritious one. The group thinks that is a great idea. Mrs. Lake agrees they could get a show of hands for each of the five products.

"If you do this," she says, "it must be within your 10-minute report period. Your trial run was slightly over 10 minutes."

"If Lieu, Bobby, and Manuel can reduce their parts by about 30 seconds each, there will be enough time for the poll at the end," states Sid.

The group members agree and then decide to run through their presentation again during lunch.

Making the progress report

As the time for their presentation draws close, each student feels nervous, never having spoken in front of such a large group. The transparencies help, since the written content will serve as cues for the presentation. The students support each other, and the presentation goes well.

The voting at the end of the presentation results in the two most popular pizzas receiving the top rankings. Sid ends by telling the audience that, at their final presentation, the most nutritious pizza will be revealed.

The group is pleased with its work. Mrs. Lake tells them that once they complete their analyses and tabulate the results, she will treat the five of them to a feast. The winning—most nutritious—pizza will be delivered. And she will be sure to provide a nutritious alternative for Nancy. Everyone applauds!

EVALUATING PROGRESS

Following the student presentations, and as feedback on their reports, Ms. Lopez schedules a review meeting with each student group. She meets with the Best Pizza Buy team two days later.

The presentation

First, she shows them how she and other teachers evaluated their presentation:

Progress Report Evaluation

OVERALL EVALUATION = 3.5

1	2	3	4
LOW			HIGH

COMMENTS

"Well organized information."

"Each student participated satisfactorily."

"Sid did a good job of bridging from one speaker to the next."

"Nancy summarized the meetings in an understandable way."

"Lieu speaks well, but needs to project her voice more."

"Bobby tends to mumble and not look at the audience."

"Manuel needs to improve his general public speaking skills."

Then Ms. Lopez discusses some details with the group, and answers such questions as:

- "Compared with other groups, how do we rate?" (In the upper third of all groups.)

- "Did you like the vote on the best pizza at the end of our report?" (A nice touch that builds interest in your project.)

The written report

Next, Ms. Lopez turns to the written progress report. A copy had been printed for each student. She has made some notes and asked a few questions for clarification. Mrs. Lake is asked for her judgment of the group's work, and she is very positive. Everyone seems pleased with the cooperation, decisions, and progress to date. The group receives a grade of B+.

Finally, Ms. Lopez wants to know how the group will proceed and what each student will do to accomplish the group's goal. Each student replies, with some assistance from the others and from Mrs. Lake.

Student journals

Then Ms. Lopez reminds the group that each person should be keeping his or her journal and portfolio collection up-to-date. She informs them that in two days she will collect and read each journal. Then she will schedule a time to meet with each student to review his or her journal and portfolio.

The meeting ends when Ms. Lopez indicates her agreement with the forthcoming activities and offers her vote for the most nutritious pizza. The group invites her to the winning pizza party!

CARRYING OUT THE ANALYSES

Now back to work. Plans are made to return to the university to conduct the analyses. A date and time are confirmed with Dr. Smith. It is decided that Mrs. Lake will purchase the five pizzas on the day of the visit. Bobby and Manuel will direct the lab work.

At the university, they are met by a graduate student from the Nutritional Science Department. Dr. Smith is at a meeting, but she has left instructions for them to go to the lab and start their work. The graduate student will help as necessary.

An assembly operation is set up:

- Lieu weighs each complete pizza on a large scale.

- Nancy and Sid separate each one's ingredients, placing different items in glass containers.

- Bobby and Manuel weigh the components on a smaller, more sensitive scale. Lieu records the data. Each measurement is double-checked for accuracy.

Once the necessary data are gathered, they all look over the results to make certain nothing has been missed. When Bobby sees the piles of pizza debris, he decides they don't look very good to eat. Like the others, he'll await the celebration, after their final presentation.

The students still want to go through some literature Dr. Smith had recommended, but the lab work is enough for one day, so they return to school.

MAKING FINAL CALCULATIONS

The next day, the group meets in the school library. Manuel is with Mrs. Sawitz at a library computer. She shows him how to use the nutritional content database program obtained from Dr. Smith. Manuel sits at the terminal and pulls up pizza food elements as Bobby calls them out for pizza sample #1 from the analysis list. Then Manuel reads off the numbers of grams per unit of ingredient. They follow this procedure for all five samples.

Once the students see the spreadsheet results, the final step is to calculate percentages of the nutritional value for each pizza sample. This will involve everyone the next day.

Bobby notes that many entry numbers are in decimals. He recalls his difficulties with learning about decimals, and he wants to show that now he can handle them. He decides to borrow the self-study program on decimals he had originally studied and to review it this evening in preparation for doing his share of the calculations.

The following day, the students tabulate the results and use the formula Dr. Smith gave them to determine percentages for nutritional content. The results look quite logical. The students decide they would like to go over their calculations with Ms.

Lopez or Mr. Sanchez. The latter agrees to meet with them.

Once the data and calculations for the five sample pizzas are completed, it is time to make comparisons and draw conclusions. To do this, the group decides to prepare a large chart.

PREPARING THE FINAL REPORT AND PRESENTATION

Mrs. Lake reminds the students that their final presentation of 15 minutes will be given, along with those of all the other groups, at an evening open house for parents, school administrators, and community representatives. Also, the group is to set up a display in a classroom, explaining their project.

Sid speaks with Mrs. Chin, the art teacher, to obtain a large sheet of cardboard and colored felt pens to make the chart. She is pleased to help them. Before starting, the group sketches out the results of the analyses on a chalkboard. When they are satisfied with the chart's appearance and have agreement on all numbers, they decide that Lieu and Bobby, both of whom can print neatly, should prepare the final, large chart. They share their layout plan with Mrs. Chin and ask her opinion of their design, lettering size, and color use.

The group agrees that the final report and the presentation should build on their work on the earlier written progress report and presentation. Now they will extend them both to include the analyses, results, and conclusions. Also, consideration is given to suggestions received when the progress report and presentation were evaluated. Knowing that parents and other adults will attend this program, each student wants the team to do a superb job.

Discussion, debating suggested ideas, and finally making decisions and assigning responsibilities takes a couple of days. Mrs. Lake is impressed with the growth exhibited by each member of the group from the start of the project. They now comprise a cooperating team, with a sincere desire to accomplish their goal.

The presentation

A storyboard is designed to organize the information. The university student who helped to prepare the transparencies for the progress report is present. Now, she suggests that presentation software such as Microsoft PowerPoint® could be used to design color slides of their results, including titles, and even a couple of cartoons scanned in from a CD-ROM art collection. The group is excited about this idea! But where can they obtain the software program, and how do they learn to use it?

The university student checks at her department and brings a PowerPoint® software CD and an art disk to help the group construct their slides. Choosing colors and slide background textures is really fun! After the images are created, they are stored on a disk. Then they can be projected directly onto a screen from computer memory via a video projector. This special use of media technology impresses the middle school students. They would all like to know more about these techniques.

Finally, the students feel that they need some help with their presentation skills. Mrs. Lake suggests that another university student give them some guidance in speaking before a group and in handling their materials. They like this idea, and during rehearsal, they receive assistance and suggestions from the university student.

The exhibit

A display is prepared, incorporating the large chart and some of the equipment used in the analyses. All project exhibits are set up in a room adjacent to the school auditorium on the afternoon before the evening presentation.

The written report

The report is developed using a word-processing and graphics software program. This allows for the selection of multisize headings, bullets for listed items, charts, artwork, and a cover design. Careful proofreading and some revisions are made in the report until it is finally approved by all.

DELIVERING THE FINAL REPORT AND PRESENTATION

Copies of the eight-page final report are made and assembled by the students. Seeing and holding this evidence of their successful project is an exciting feeling for everyone. This motivates them further to make a good presentation.

"Boy!" says Manuel. "This is just like *Consumer Reports,* when they rate foods and other products. Maybe they'd like to see our research and publish it in their magazine!"

The evening of the open house brings a large turnout of parents (including the Martins and Mrs. Hester), most of the teachers from Stoneridge, school administrators, three school board members, college students who assisted with projects, some professors (including Dr. Lewis, the program facilitator, and Dr. Smith), and a number of community representatives.

As people arrive, they spend time looking over the students' exhibits of their projects. Two members of the Best Pizza Buy team stay with their display to explain and answer questions. The rest of the team visit and react to other team projects. Every 15 minutes, they rotate responsibilities. Also, they check the set-up of the computer, video projector, and screen in the auditorium.

Everyone who attends, including students, is given a short form for judging each display. The evaluative criteria are to determine how well the team (1) describes its goal, procedures, results, and conclusions; (2) has designed the display to communicate information; and (3) makes the display attractive.

After a general greeting in the auditorium from Mrs. Stefans, the principal, the teachers involved in the new program introduce each team of students for its presentation. Each project is evaluated by all Stoneridge teachers present.

There is applause at the end of each team presentation. The Best Pizza Buy team receives extra acclaim when, at the end, Sid Grant announces the name of the winning pizza!

After the program concludes, the Best Pizza Buy team students go to their exhibit, complimenting each other and joking about the great job they have done. The parents of each student join them, expressing their pleasure with the team's work. Mrs. Lake asks if the students are ready for their pizza treat. Mrs. Stefans offers to buy pizzas for the parents, so everyone can celebrate together. ◆

REFERENCES AND SOURCES

A. MOVING INTO THE 21ST CENTURY (CHAPTERS 1, 2)

Banathy, B. *Systems Design of Education: A Journey to Create the Future.* Englewood Cliffs, NJ: Educational Technology Publications, 1991.

Boulding, K. E. *The World as a Total System.* Beverly Hills, CA: Sage, 1985.

Deming, W. E. *The New Economics for Industry, Government, Education.* Cambridge, MA: MIT, Center for Advanced Engineering Study, 1993.

Drucker, P. *Post-Capitalist Society.* New York: HarperBusiness, 1993.

Johnston, W. B., and Packer, A. H. *Workforce 2000: Work and Workers for the Twenty-First Century.* Indianapolis: Hudson Institute, 1987.

McBeath, R. J. "Is Education Becoming?" *AudioVisual Communications Review* (Spring 1969): 36–40.

Naisbitt, H., and Aburdene, P. *Megatrends 2000: Ten New Directions for the 1990s.* New York: Morrow, 1990.

Senge, P. M. *The Fifth Discipline.* New York: Doubleday, 1990.

Toffler, A. *Future Shock.* New York: Random House, 1970.

———. *The Third Wave.* New York: Morrow, 1980.

———. *Powershift.* New York: Bantam Books, 1990.

What Work Requires of Schools: A SCANS Report for America 2000. Washington, DC: U.S. Department of Labor, 1991.

Whitaker, K. S., and Moses, M. C. *The Restructuring Handbook: A Guide to School Revitalization.* Needham Heights, MA: Allyn & Bacon, 1994.

B. THE CHANGE PROCESS (CHAPTERS 2, 3, 6)

Allen, D. W. *Schools for a New Century: A Conservative Approach to Radical School Reform.* New York: Praeger, 1992.

Bullard, P., and Taylor, B. O. *Making School Reform Happen.* Needham Heights, MA: Allyn & Bacon, 1993.

An Educators' Guide to Schoolwide Reform. Arlington, VA: Educational Research Service, 1999.

ERS Informed Educator: Managing Change in Education. Arlington, VA: Educational Research Service, 1998.

Fullan, M. G., with Suzanne Stiegelbauer. *The New Meaning of Educational Change.* New York: Teachers College Press, Columbia University, 1991.

Fullan, M. G. *Change Forces: The Sequel.* Philadelphia: Falmer Press, 1999.

Gainey, D. D. *Education for the New Century: Views from the Principal's Office.* Reston, VA: National Association of Secondary School Principals, 1993.

Gelinas, M. V., and James, R. C. *Developing the Foundation for Change.* Washington, DC: International Society for Performance Improvement, 1996.

Hanushek, E. A. *Making Schools Work.* Washington, DC: The Brookings Institution, 1994.

Havelock, R. G., with Steve Zlotolow. *The Change Agent's Guide.* Englewood Cliffs, NJ: Educational Technology Publications, 1995.

Kaufman, R. A. *Mapping Educational Success: Strategic Thinking and Planning for School Administrators.* Thousand Oaks, CA: Corwin Press, 1995.

Lieberman, A. (Ed.). *Building a Professional Culture in Schools.* New York: Teachers College Press, Columbia University, 1988.

Mehlinger, H. D. *School Reform in the Information Age.* Bloomington, IN: Center for Excellence in Education, Indiana University, 1995.

Murphy, J., and Schiller, J. *Transforming America's Schools: An Administrators'* [sic] *Call to Action.* La-Salle, IL: Open Court, 1992.

Newmann, F., and Wehlage, G. *Successful School Restructuring: A Report to the Public and Educators.* Madison, WI: Wisconsin Center for Educational Research, 1995.

Perelman, L. J. *School's Out!* New York: Morrow, 1992.

Salisbury, D. F. *Five Technologies for Educational Change.* Englewood Cliffs, NJ: Educational Technology Publications, 1996.

Saxl, E. R., et al. *Assisting Change in Education: A Training Program for School Improvement Facilitators.* Alexandria, VA: Association for Supervision and Curriculum Development, 1989.

Senge, P. M. *The Fifth Discipline Fieldbook: Strategies and Tools for Building a Learning Organization.* New York: Doubleday, 1994.

———. *The Dance of Change: The Challenges of Sustaining Momentum in Learning Organizations.* New York: Doubleday, 1999.

Tosti, D. T. "Systemic Change." *Performance Improvement* 39, no. 3 (March 2000): 53–59.

Wilson, K. G., and Daviss, B. *Redesigning Education.* New York: Henry Holt, 1994.

C. LEARNING NEEDS (CHAPTERS 5, 6)

English, F. W., and Kaufman, R. *Needs Assessment: A Focus for Curriculum Development.* Washington, DC: Association for Supervision and Curriculum Development, 1975.

Stufflebeam, D. L., et al. *Conducting Educational Needs Assessments.* Boston: Kluwer-Nijhoff, 1985.

D. LEARNER CHARACTERISTICS (CHAPTERS 6, 10)

Bloom, B. S. *Human Characteristics and School Learning.* New York: McGraw-Hill, 1976.

Butler, K. A. *Learning Styles: Personal Exploration and Practical Applications* (Teacher Guide and Student Guide). Columbia, CT: Learner's Dimension, 1995.

Gardner, H. *Frames of Mind: The Theory of Multiple Intelligences.* New York: Basic Books, 1993.

Lawrence, G. *People Types and Tiger Stripes: A Practical Guide to Learning Styles.* Gainesville, FL: Center for Applications of Psychological Type, 1993.

Mager, R. F. *How To Turn Learners On . . . Without Turning Them Off.* Atlanta: Center for Effective Performance, 1997.

E. SYSTEMATIC INSTRUCTIONAL PLANNING (CHAPTERS 3, 8, 9)

Dick, W., and Carey, L. *The Systematic Design of Instruction.* New York: HarperCollins, 1996.

Harless, J. *The Eden Conspiracy: Educating for Accomplished Citizenship.* Wheaton, IL: Guild V Publications, 1998.

Jenlink, P. M., et al. *Facilitating Systematic Change in School Districts: A Guidebook.* Bloomington, IN: Systematic Change Agency, 1997.

Kemp, J. E., et al. *Designing Effective Instruction.* Upper Saddle River, NJ: Merrill, 1998.

———. *The Instructional Design Process.* New York: Harper & Row, 1985.

Mager, R. F. *Making Instruction Work.* Atlanta: Center for Effective Performance, 1997.

Reigeluth, C. M., and Garfinkle, R. J. (Eds.). *Systemic Change in Education.* Englewood Cliffs, NJ: Educational Technology Publications, 1994.

Reiser, R. A., and Dick, W. *Instructional Planning: A Guide for Teachers.* Needham Heights, MA: Allyn & Bacon, 1996.

Seels, B., and Glasgow, Z. *Making Instructional Design Decisions.* Upper Saddle River, NJ: Merrill, 1998.

F. CURRICULUM DEVELOPMENT (CHAPTERS 7, 8, 9)

Dirkx, J. M., and Prenger, S. M. *A Guide for Planning and Implementing Instruction for Adults: A Theme-Based Approach.* San Francisco: Jossey-Bass, 1997.

Erickson, H. L. *Stirring the Head, Heart, and Soul.* Thousand Oaks, CA: Corwin Press, 1995.

Jacobs, H. H. (Ed.). *Interdisciplinary Curriculum: Design and Implementation.* Alexandria, VA: Association for Supervision and Curriculum Development, 1989.

Jones, B. F., et al. *Real-Life Problem Solving: A Collaborative Approach to Interdisciplinary Learning.* Washington, DC: American Psychological Association, 1997.

Roberts, P. L., and Kellough, R. D. *A Guide for Developing an Interdisciplinary Thematic Unit.* Englewood Cliffs, NJ: Merrill, 1996.

G. Learning objectives (Chapter 8)

Bloom, B. S. (Ed.). *Taxonomy of Educational Objectives: Handbook I. Cognitive Domain*. New York: Longman, 1984.

Harrow, A. J. *A Taxonomy of the Psychomotor Domain*. New York: David McKay, 1972.

Krathwohl, D. R., et al. *Taxonomy of Educational Objectives: Handbook II. The Affective Domain*. New York: Longman, 1984.

Mager, R. F. *Developing Attitude toward Learning*. Palo Alto, CA: Fearon, 1968.

————. *Preparing Instructional Objectives*. Atlanta: Center for Effective Performance, 1997.

Martin, B. L., and Briggs, L. J. *The Affective and Cognitive Domains: Integration for Instruction and Research*. Englewood Cliffs, NJ: Educational Technology Publications, 1986.

H. Instructional and learning methods (Chapter 9)

Adams, D., et al. *Cooperative Learning and Educational Media: Collaborating with Technology and Each Other*. Englewood Cliffs, NJ: Educational Technology Publications, 1990.

Caine, R. N., and Caine, G. *Making Connections: Teaching and the Human Brain*. Alexandria, VA: Association for Supervision and Curriculum Development, 1991.

Cohen, E. G. *Designing Groupwork: Strategies for the Heterogeneous Classroom*. New York: Teachers College Press, Columbia University, 1994.

Glasser, W. *Alternative Strategies to Social Promotion*. Port Chester, NY: National Professional Resources, 1998.

Integrating the Curriculum Videotapes—#1 (41 min.); *#2* (20 min.). Palatine, IL: IRI/Skylight, 1994.

Jacobs, H. H. (Ed.). *Interdisciplinary Curriculum: Design and Implementation*. Alexandria, VA: Association for Supervision and Curriculum Development, 1989.

Jenkins, J. M., and Tanner, D. *Restructuring for an Interdisciplinary Curriculum*. Reston, VA: National Association of Secondary School Principals, 1992.

Kagan, S., and Kagan, L. *Reaching Standards through Cooperative Learning* (video series). Port Chester, NY: National Professional Resources, 2000.

Maeroff, G. I. *Team Building for School Change*. New York: Teachers College Press, Columbia University, 1993.

Marzano, R. *A Different Kind of Classroom: Teaching with Dimensions of Learning*. Alexandria, VA: Association for Supervision and Curriculum Development, 1992.

McBeath, R. J. *Instructing and Evaluating in Higher Education: A Guidebook for Planning Learning Outcomes*. Englewood Cliffs, NJ: Educational Technology Publications, 1992.

Meeks, K., and Stauffer, M. C. *Closing the Achievement Gap*. Port Chester, NY: National Professional Resources, 2000.

Odyssey of the Mind. *http://www.odysseyofthemind.org*.

Schipper, B., and Rossi, J. *Portfolios in the Classroom*. York, ME: Stenhouse, 1997.

Shortt, T. L., and Thayer, Y. V. *The Complete Handbook of Block Scheduling: Success for Students and Teachers through Efficient Use of Time and Human Resources*. Bloomington, IN: TECHNOS Press of the Agency for Instructional Technology, 1999.

Slavin, R. E. *Cooperative Learning: Theory, Research, and Practice*. Needham Heights, MA: Allyn & Bacon, 1995.

Vars, G. F. *Interdisciplinary Teaching in the Middle Grades: Why and How*. Columbus, OH: National Middle School Association, 1987.

Wiles, B. *Designing Interdisciplinary Units*. Tampa, FL: Wiles Bondi & Associates, 1988.

————. *Teaming in the Middle School*. Tampa, FL: Wiles Bondi & Associates, 1990.

I. Instructional resources (Chapter 10)

Badgett, T., and Sandler, C. *Welcome to the Internet: From Mystery to Mastery*. New York: MIS Press, 1993.

Bix, C., et al. *Kids Do the Web*. Berkeley, CA: Peachpit Press/Adobe Press, 1996.

Brody, P. J. *Technology Planning and Management Handbook*. Englewood Cliffs, NJ: Educational Technology Publications, 1995.

Clark, D. *Student's Guide to the Internet*. Indianapolis: Alpha Books, 1995.

Craver, K. W. *School Library Media Centers in the 21st Century.* Westport, CT: Greenwood Press, 1994.

Dockterman, D. A. *Great Teaching in the One-Computer Classroom.* Watertown, MA: Tom Snyder Productions, 1991.

Donham, J. *Enhancing Teaching and Learning: A Leadership Guide for School Library Media Specialists.* New York: Neal-Schuman, 1998.

Electronic Learning journal. New York: Scholastic, Inc.

Frick, T. W. *Restructuring Education through Technology.* Fastback #326. Bloomington, IN: Phi Delta Kappa Educational Foundation, 1991.

Gooden, A. R. *Computers in the Classroom: How Teachers and Students are Using Technology to Transform Learning.* San Francisco: Jossey-Bass/Apple Press, 1996.

Heinich, R., et al. *Educational Media and Technologies for Learning.* Upper Saddle River, NJ: Merrill, 1999.

Improving Education through Distributed Learning (Program Guide 1999–2000). Downey, CA: Los Angeles County Office of Education, 1999.

Kemp, J. E., and Smellie, D. C. *Planning, Producing, and Using Instructional Technologies.* New York: HarperCollins, 1994.

Means, B., et al. *Using Technology to Support Education Reform.* Washington, DC: U.S. Department of Education, Office of Educational Research and Improvement, Office of Research, 1993.

Ohio Schools Technology Implementation Task Force. *http://www.ohioschoolnet.k12.oh.us/home/.*

Project CHILD (Computers Helping Instruction and Learning Development). Tallahassee, FL: Institute for School Innovation, Inc. *http://www.ifsi.org/child.htm.*

Schank, R. C., and Cleary, C. *Engines for Education.* Hillsdale, NJ: Lawrence Erlbaum Associates, 1995.

Schrum, L., and Luetkehans, L. *A Primer on Distance Education.* Washington, DC: Association for Educational Communications and Technology, 1997.

J. EVALUATION OF LEARNING (CHAPTER 12)

Kohn, A. *The Schools Our Children Deserve: Moving Beyond Traditional Classrooms and "Tougher Standards."* Boston: Houghton Mifflin, 1999.

Kubiszyn, T., and Borich, G. D. *Educational Testing and Measurement.* New York: HarperCollins, 1996.

Mager, R. F. *Measuring Instructional Results.* Atlanta: Center for Effective Performance, 1997.

Paulson, F. L., and Paulson, P. R. *A Guide for Judging Portfolios.* Portland, OR: Multnomah Educational Service District, 1994.

Popham, W. J. *Educational Evaluation.* Englewood Cliffs, NJ: Prentice-Hall, 1988.

K. SUMMATIVE EVALUATION (CHAPTER 13)

Berk, R. A., and Rossi, P. H. *Thinking about Program Evaluation.* Newbury Park, CA: Sage, 1990.

Herman, J. L., and Winters, L. *Tracking Your School's Success: A Guide to Sensible Evaluation.* Newbury Park, CA: Corwin Press, 1992.

Morris, L. L., et al. *How to Communicate Evaluation Findings.* Newbury Park, CA: Sage, 1987.

Phillips, J. J. *Return on Investment in Training and Performance Improvement Programs.* Houston: Gulf, 1997.

Rutman, L. *Planning Useful Evaluations.* Beverly Hills, CA: Sage, 1980.

L. PROGRAM MANAGEMENT (CHAPTERS 10, 11, 12, 13, 14)

Becoming a School Partner: A Guidebook for Organizing Intergenerational Partnerships in Schools. Washington, DC: American Association of Retired People, 1996.

Bennett, W. J. *The Educated Child: A Parent's Guide from Preschool through Eighth Grade.* New York: The Free Press, 1999.

Bullard, P., and Taylor, B. O. *Making School Reform Happen.* Needham, MA: Allyn & Bacon, 1993.

Every Student Succeeds: A Conceptual Framework for Students at Risk of School Failure. Sacramento, CA: California Department of Education, 1994.

Gainey, D. D. *Education for the New Century: Views from the Principal's Office.* Reston, VA: National Association of Secondary School Principals, 1993.

Havelock, R. G., with Steve Zlotolow. *The Change Agent's Guide.* Englewood Cliffs, NJ: Educational Technology Publications, 1995.

Kaufman, R. A. *Auditing Your Educational Strategic Plan: Making a Good Thing Better.* Thousand Oaks, CA: Corwin Press, 1995.

Klein, S., et al. *Studies of Education Reform. Fitting the Pieces: Education Reform That Works.* Washington, DC: U.S. Department of Education, Office of Educational Research and Improvement, Office of Reform Assistance and Dissemination, 1996.

Ladd, H. F. (Ed.). *Holding Schools Accountable: Performance-Based Reform in Education.* Washington, DC: The Brookings Institution, 1996.

A Leader's Guide to School Restructuring. Reston, VA: National Association of Secondary School Principals, 1992.

Otterbourg, S. D. *A Business Guide to Support Employees and Family Involvement in Education.* New York: The Conference Board, 1997.

Warner, C. *Everybody's House—The Schoolhouse: Best Techniques for Connecting Home, School, and Community.* Thousand Oaks, CA: Corwin Press, 1997.

M. SUCCESSFUL INNOVATIVE SCHOOL PROJECTS

Bullard, P., and Taylor, B. O. *Making School Reform Happen.* Needham Heights, MA: Allyn & Bacon, 1993.

Comer, J. P. (Ed.). *Rallying the Whole Village: The Comer Process for Reforming Education.* New York: Teachers College Press, Columbia University, 1996.

———. *Reinventing Our Schools.* (video), Bloomington, IN: Agency for Instructional Technology, 1994.

Comprehensive Models for School Improvement: Finding the Right Match and Making It Work. Arlington, VA: Educational Research Service, 1998.

Finnan, C. (Ed.). *Accelerated Schools in Action.* Thousand Oaks, CA: Corwin Press, 1996.

Klein, S., et al. *Studies of Education Reform. Fitting the Pieces: Education Reform That Works.* Washington, DC: U.S. Department of Education, Office of Educational Research and Improvement, Office of Reform Assistance and Dissemination, 1996.

Levin, H. M. *Learning from Accelerated Schools.* Philadelphia: Pew Charitable Trusts, 1991.

New American Schools Development Corporation (NASDC). *Vision to Reality: Tomorrow's Schools Today.* Washington, DC: NASDC, 1994.

Project CHILD (Computers Helping Instruction and Learning Development). Tallahassee, FL: Institute for School Innovation, Inc. *http://www.ifsi.org/child.htm.*

Sizer, H. *Horace's Compromise: The Dilemma of the American High School.* Boston: Houghton Mifflin, 1984.

———. *Horace's School: Redesigning the American High School.* Boston: Houghton Mifflin, 1992.

Slavin, R. E. *Every Child, Every School: Success for All.* Thousand Oaks, CA: Corwin, 1996.

Slavin, R. E., et al. (Eds.). *Preventing Early School Failure: Research, Policy, and Practice.* Needham Heights, MA: Allyn & Bacon, 1994.

Stringfield, S., et al. *Bold Plans for School Restructuring: The New American Schools Designs.* Mahwah, NJ: Lawrence Erlbaum Associates, 1996.

Wood, G. *Schools That Work.* New York: Dutton, 1992.

N. GRANT SOURCE INFORMATION

The Chronicle of Philanthropy. 202/466-1200 or *http://www.philanthropy.com/.*

Council on Foundations. 1828 K Street, N.W., Suite 300, Washington, DC 20036.

The Directory of Corporate Foundation Givers. 800/877-8238 (Taft Group) or 800/877-4253 (Gale Group) to order.

Education Funding Research Council, 1725 K Street, 7th Floor, Washington, DC 20006.

Education Grants Alert. Frederick, MD: Aspen Publishers. 800/638-8437 or *http://www.aspenpublishers.com.*

The Foundation Directory. The Foundation Center. 800/424-9836 or *http://www.fdncenter.org/.*

Grants Net Project. Division of Grants Policy and Oversight, U.S. Department of Health and Human Services. *http://www.hhs.gov/grantsnet/.*

Grant Seekers Guide: A Guide to Federal Program Officers. Frederick, MD: Aspen Publishers. 800/638-8437 or *http://www.aspenpublishers.com.*

Polaris Corporation. 800/368-3775.

INDEX

Curriculum topics, 22, 39–41
    basic skills, 40
    interdisciplinary themes, 40
    problem-based projects, 40–41
    subject disciplines, 40